THE SPACE OF LIFE
BETWEEN

THE SPACE OF LIFE BETWEEN

By
Fr. BEDE JARRETT, o.p.

NEW YORK
SHEED & WARD
1943

NIHIL OBSTAT: FR. CHRYSOSTOMUS EGAN, O.P.
FR. ROBERTUS BRACEY, O.P.
NIHIL OBSTAT: GEORGIUS D. SMITH, S.T.D.
CENSOR DEPUTATUS
IMPRIMATUR: EDM: CAN: SURMONT
VIC: GEN.
WESTMONASTERII, DIE 31 MARTII 1930

FIRST PUBLISHED, APRIL 1930
BY SHEED AND WARD LTD.
110/111 FLEET STREET
LONDON, E.C.4
THIRD IMPRESSION, 1943

BOOK PRODUCTION WAR ECONOMY STANDARD

THE PAPER AND BINDING
OF THIS BOOK CONFORMS
TO THE AUTHORISED ECONOMY STANDARD

PRINTED IN GREAT BRITAIN BY
LOWE AND BRYDONE PRINTERS LIMITED, LONDON, N.W.10

CONTENTS

	page
A LETTER IN DEDICATION	9
1. GOD	17
2. GOD'S PRESENCE	20
3. GOD'S SON	23
4. ETERNAL LIFE	26
5. THE SON OF GOD	29
6. JESUS MOST LOVABLE	32
7. LIFE AND LOVE	35
8. SOURCES OF LIFE	38
9. INDIVIDUALITY	42
10. OUR CALLING	46
11. THE PRIESTHOOD	50
12. MY CAREER	54
13. SELF-INDULGENCE	58
14. WOMEN	62
15. LOVE	66
16. MARRIAGE	70
17. FRIENDSHIP	74
18. WINE	78
19. PURITY	82
20. OUR LADY	86
21. TOWER OF IVORY	90
22. FAITHFUL VIRGIN	94
23. HEALTH OF THE WEAK	98

		page
24.	LOVE OF LIFE	102
25.	GOD'S WILL	106
26.	CIRCUMSTANCES	110
27.	MY ROOM	114
28.	GAMES	118
29.	VANITY	122
30.	HYPOCRISY	126
31.	WORK	130
32.	THESE DEGENERATE DAYS	134
33.	COURAGE	138
34.	HONOUR	142
35.	HEAVEN	146
36.	HELL	151
37.	PURGATORY	155
38.	DEATH	160
39.	HAPPINESS	165
40.	ANGELS	170
41.	SAINTS	175
42.	IDEALS	179
43.	LOYALTY	183
44.	MIRACLES	187
45.	LAW	191

The imagination of a boy is healthy, and the mature imagination of a man is healthy; but there is a SPACE OF LIFE BETWEEN, *in which the soul is in a ferment, the character undecided, the way of life uncertain, the ambition thick-sighted: thence proceeds mawkishness, and all the thousand bitters which those men I speak of must necessarily taste.*

KEATS, in the preface to *Endymion*.

A LETTER IN DEDICATION

DEAR CHRISTOPHER,

You will be surprised to have a letter from me, and even more surprised to have a book. But when I was little like you, I liked letters and books if only they had pictures in them, for I was often lucky enough to have letters sent me full of pictures, sometimes drawn on the paper, sometimes stuck on.

Well, this letter will have a picture, though not drawn in or even stuck on the paper; the picture I want to send is a picture of your father whom, perhaps, you will never remember having seen, but who is wonderfully worth remembering if you can remember him at all. A boy he was when I first knew him: tall, slim, with a charming character; beautiful manners he had, ready to do anything for anybody, but yet with a will of his own. Indeed, one of my early recollections of him is seeing him with a 'black eye'. That was soon after the War had broken out, and he had entered a cadet corps. There were all sorts of people in with him: people who had all sorts of ideas and ways. Their language was not always clean, nor their ideas, and their views of Catholic doctrine were rather ignorant. Well, somehow something had been said against the Mother of God and her purity. The 'black eye' was the result he suffered; I never saw what befell the other man. But that was your father's way; Ben we called him: very quiet till he was roused, and then he remained quiet, but he did what he thought he should.

His only defect was a temptation to be diffident and scrupulous. Many a talk I have had with him in the garden of S. Dominic's, in North-West London, his coming preceded by a telegram; I knew it meant several hours exercise, endless walking round and round our garden, and always the subject discussed to be some instance of scrupulous diffidence. He was by that time in the Flying Corps, and though he had passed the various tests, he never could believe that he was fit to fly. He just loved flying and was ready to go by himself to the world's end; but he was terrified of taking up anyone else. He felt sure he would be endangering their lives. Ought he not to give up flying? He would never be fit for anything else, he said. A priest, perhaps, he might be, so long as he was a religious, but he did not really feel that he was meant for that way of service.

Then, of course, he was cured at last, because he found your mother. She healed him of his troubles by her intrepid faith in God and her confidence in him. Those two strong things in her character gave him his peace. After he had decided to marry her and she had agreed, he was never really distressed again, though he had his hard life to follow, the little family, the small pay of the officer, himself pressed into the part of nurserymaid when the official one had her 'afternoon off'. But your mother's love and faith and confidence fitted into him and made him the fine soul he now swiftly became: gentle and courteous and full of fun, and radiant always, with his scruples forgotten, wholly free.

What has all this to do with this book? Really it had everything to do with it. Your father did everything except the actual writing of it. All the idea of it, and even many of the ideas in it, were his. It happened this way.

I was giving a retreat at the convent of Grayshott, and your mother was there attending it. Your father determined to fly over and call on her and on me; they were not yet married, but were very soon to be married. He came at any rate and found lodgings in the village and crept into a gallery in the Chapel and heard one of the sermons of the retreat, and then had supper with me afterwards. Again he heard a second sermon after supper, and then came to my room and talked. Why was nothing done for young men? That was the burden of his complaint. Children had books written for them, and nuns, and priests, and fully grown up and steady folk all were spiritually catered for; why did no one write anything for young men? I answered that there was little use writing books for young men because they would not read the books and already didn't; his reply was that this was his precise complaint. Of course, they did not read them because none of the books were suited to them. So there was never any use reading them. They would read if they only had the right books.

I had still two other arguments, namely that by the time one became a priest venturing to write, one's generation was already getting old and out of touch with youth. Only the young knew the young, hence I was now out of the race. You can guess that by this time he had made it a personal question: why did not I write this book? My other answer was that I was rather afraid of young men: they seemed to me so wonderful and even magnificent that I never thought they would pay attention to what I wrote. He blazed out at this and said on the contrary they were extraordinarily shy and were only too pleased if anyone paid attention spiritually to them, that they were the most forlorn folk in the Kingdom of God, too self-conscious to speak, too sensitive to religious ideals to want to escape religion, too tempted to move simply with the sacraments, too perplexed always to see their way.

At last it was getting so late that I had to pack him off into the warm summer darkness, the fragrance of the night flowers mingling with the gentle light of the half-hid stars; the last thing I shouted down the road after him was that I would do the book if he would tell me what he wanted done in it.

Next morning he was at Mass and Communion, and shared with me the prodigious breakfast always provided by the nuns; we had hardly begun it before he produced out of his waistcoat pocket his calling card with a list of subjects scribbled on the back of it. He had worked it all out overnight since after our long talk he had felt so much awake that sleep was impossible. After breakfast he fled off to his aerodrome again, leaving me this token and the request to do it for his sake.

THE SPACE OF LIFE BETWEEN

If you do remember your father, you will know why I had to agree.

After some months I finished the Meditations (that is what in the end he asked for) on the list as he had given it to me, and added a few of my own. He had agreed to read it through and criticize it when the book was finished. I had almost finished it when he had that accident, when he was flying in India, which took him from you till one day, please God, you shall see him again. Since then I have never wanted to look at my manuscript. His going made a greater gap in many other lives than in my own, no doubt; but the gap it made in mine was sufficient for me not to want to have more reminders of him, active, brimming with life, talking hard, bursting with humour, frank, free, than I need have. He was dead; yet who could think of him except as vividly alive?

Then, my dear Christopher, your photograph was shown me: one taken in your Surrey garden. Rather a stout little fellow you look in it, with a wide smile; he was slim, dark, lithe, brown-eyed, wide-shouldered, tall like his father and mother before him. Then I thought that as I owed it to him to fulfill my promise, and since he was no longer here to receive what thus I owed him, you as his heir, were the proper person to whom the debt should be paid.

I have not had the heart properly to finish the book; as it was when he went, so I give it to you. Do not think of it except as somehow his. Pray for me sometimes when you have prayed for him; I shall feel immeasurably repaid if you will do that.

Gather memories of him from your mother when you can, and grow to the stature of these memories as she holds them; if you do, you will find life hard, perhaps, but you will find it to be life indeed. May He that kept Ben close to Him keep you also as near to Him as Ben was; then when you come to your ending you will surely see him in that greater Father who begot him and you.

> Your affectionate friend,
> FATHER BEDE JARRETT, O.P.

GOD

I

WE must always begin with God as we must end with Him. From Him we came and to Him we go. This divine ancestry and divine destiny of ours is none of our doing; it happens to us whether we will or no. But what is to happen in the years between our coming and our going? Shall we be with God then? Here we come on something that does lie with us to settle. We can then determine for ourselves whether we keep by Him or not. Rather, perhaps, we ought to say, not that we can determine to keep by Him, but only that we can determine to open our eyes to His presence, for we are kept by Him whether we will or no. He made us and will receive us at the end, and is with us all our lives, so that upon us rests only the choice of determining whether we shall be conscious of that presence or ignore it. We cannot make away with it. It steadily and for ever abides, but what shall we do with it?

II

To answer this we must first note that we have one great desire always, and that is to live. We desire life. Even when, under stress of grief or failure or pain we cry out for death, it is only because our distress makes us realise how life is denied us by grief or failure or pain; these do not necessarily shorten existence, but if we surrender to them they quench something of the thrill and stir of life. Life is indeed our desire. We turn then, variously, according to our temperament or experience, to what we think will give us life. Under whatever guise or disguise we fancy it to be, we still pursue it. The crowd in the streets, the line of lamps, the wet pavements reflecting the lights, music, the dance, the play, or the sounds and sights of nature in the country, or the companionship of books, or art, or friends, these according to each one's taste, may seem for the moment to be life's most attractive form, most vital, most energizing. But whichever at any time most appeals to us, does so precisely because it seems most vividly to be filled with life.

III

Now God is life. He is indeed the Creator of all living things; they are His, and have through Him their being and movement. But more than this, mysteriously He shares with them this wonderful life. It is a participation by them in His being, without loss to Him, of course, without impinging on His essence, without at all breaking in on His incommunicable divinity. Yet truly He is life; so truly that He gave it as the name by which He should be known to the children of Israel; I AM WHO AM, which is the very fulness of life. Being, existence, crammed to the edge and limit of it with activity, is the nearest we can get—and even then quite inadequately—to our imagination of God. He has no limits; not then as life, that is pent and glowing, but as wholly without anything to narrow Him, we must conceive of Him and try to realize Him within us, endlessly, a perpetual source of life.

GOD'S PRESENCE

I

BECAUSE God is life, we are made more alive by being conscious of His presence. We desire life: also we need it. We desire it, and under many forms pursue it, and if we did not we should die. Men do so die, who have deliberately laid aside desire for living. In illness, when it reaches that moment of crisis, whence slopes in either direction life or death, much depends on the desire of the patient for either choice. If he really has no desire for living, gives in, is listless, will not put up a fight for life, his case is already hopeless. It is more often the spirit than the body that decides between living and surrendering life. A man can refuse to surrender himself, make violent efforts against the attacks made on him and eagerly throw such energies of mind as remain to him into every remedy proposed, contest every failing breath, drive with each heartbeat a fresh supply of blood through all his veins, and fight his way steadily and without recoil back into the paths of health. Even without illness, a man can let himself lose vitality by making no contrary effort. He can acquiese in and encourage and hasten his end.

II

Life, therefore, must be fought for. Despite our normal thoughts of it, as something wholly independent of us, it does in some measure fall under our power; so, too, in some measure does God. He too is life, and in that shape lives similarly at our mercy. We can live through Him or fail to live at all. His presence is indeed within us, whether we will or not; but we have this left to us, that we can keep conscious of His presence or ignore it. We can refuse to remember that He lies at the centre of our soul, or we can have the blessedness of arriving at a state when we know that we walk with God: nor need this be a mere passing mood, it can be a continuous experience; not exactly that we deliberately and directly think of God the whole time, but that we are never really far from Him at any time. Just as sometimes, when we know beforehand

THE SPACE OF LIFE BETWEEN

that something happy is to come to us during the day, we have a happy feeling in all we do, without directly remembering what makes us happy, so can the consciousness of God's presence infuse itself into our temper of mind.

III

Is it possible for the ordinary man to have this consciousness ? Would it not destroy the pleasure of exercise, of friendship, of work and amusements ? Would we not become too solemn for our part in the world ? Not at all. Frequently quite ordinary men of any age have it and are not the less, but the more, happy for having it. It is merely the result of an intense though brief act of the presence of God made in morning prayers, in night prayers, and at middle-day. Nothing more complicated is needed than that. The consciousness will grow of itself from these three moments and become so habitual as to intwine itself with all our acts and thoughts, and give an unconscious refinement to our views and dreams.

GOD'S SON

I

THE living presence of God that gives us life cannot however usually be experienced directly. [It is only through faith that we come to a knowledge either of God or of His presence.] We cannot prove this presence of God, for the emotions or feelings which we sometimes experience and which seem to convince us of it are not real proofs of it at all. They may be due as much to external circumstances as to our inner spirit, for it is of the very nature of these emotions which seem to give us direct knowledge of God, that they should depend upon conditions of health or weather, or perhaps upon a great trial or a great joy or on the influence of others—upon things, that is, which make the proof no proof at all. We experience God by faith, and by faith only. We have no deeper knowledge of Him that comes by faith and is illumined by faith.

II

How do I know God through faith? I know all that I do know about Him through the revelation of His Son. It was God the Son, made Man, who came on earth not only to redeem the world, but to give it saving truth. He was the truth and He came to teach truth. Now the truth that He taught was nothing else than the knowledge of God, of God's dealing with man, of God's providence, judgements, rewards and punishments, and of the way to God. He revealed to us the Father. He revealed to us that this Father had care of the whole world, because He was in the world, present in every part of it. The world is His because He made it; but besides making it, He guides it; and besides guiding it, He is in it. The knowledge then of this presence of God all the world over, shown already, indeed, in the Old Testament, was reinforced by Our Lord's doctrine and by His example. Everywhere we find Him openly appealing to His Father to support His preaching, to confirm it by signs, because the Father was everywhere present, needing no prayer to make Him aware of His Son's travail, constantly beside Him. This is the particular revelation of Christ that was fresh to the world, the ubiquity of God not as a stern judge but as a kind Father.

III

Very naturally in Our Lord's mind it was this teaching which was to be the source of life to all that would hear Him: 'He that believeth in Me shall not die for ever' (John ii, 26). His words were life, and He was Himself the life, and in Him was life. His flesh and blood were instruments of life, and without these as the food of the soul, it could have no life. The sacrament of initiation into the kingdom was 'a new birth', because through it a new life was bestowed on the soul. Its waters were 'living waters', because they led to the life-giving doctrine of God's fatherhood and of His benign and eager presence so close to man and so devoted to his interests. Our Lord, therefore, very plainly conveyed by His words that the presence of God in the world and our consciousness of it would give us a share in the 'eternal life' of God, not hereafter only, but even here in this passing pilgrimage.

ETERNAL LIFE

I

We are foolishly inclined to limit the words 'eternal life' to the world beyond the grave. We are justified indeed in looking upon eternity as wholly different from time, and therefore as impossible to us in this present existence; yet it is none the less true that we are to begin our eternal life here on earth. To begin an eternity may seem a contradiction, for eternity should have neither beginning nor end; but if the human spirit is to have eternal life at all, it must enter into it, begin it in that sense, though really it does not begin eternal life, but rather the life of God that is shared with the soul plunges it into a state that is eternal. Well, then, though we are only plunged into eternity after death, the same life that shall animate us then can already begin its work here. 'As a tree falls so shall it lie,' is the wise man's judgement on life and death. What the next life brings is then a continuation, a completion of this life.

II

Now eternal life is obtained through Our Lord. He is the sole Mediator. We can reach the Father through Him alone. But how do we reach Him? To become one with the Father, we must be one with the Son. But how do we become one with the Son? How, indeed, do we become one with anybody? By becoming one with a person, we mean entering into so close a friendship with him that our ideas coincide, that our hearts work in common sympathy, our likes and dislikes are the same, that we have the same ideals, hopes, ambitions. Oneness is achieved by love and by love only. Hate separates and love unites. Consequently when we repeat the Scriptural phrases about becoming 'one with Christ' we really mean that what we aim at is a union of love with Him so close and constant that His ideas become ours, His likes and dislikes, His preferences also ours. We love Him not emotionally, at least not necessarily with emotion, but with will and intellect, with a strenuous attempt to be His followers.

III

Now this is eternal life; it is the accumulation of vital force in the soul through friendship with the sole medium of life to us. God is life as well as love. By love of Him, therefore, we are made one with Him, we are lifted to His plane of thought, we take over His judgements on pain and suffering and sorrow, we accept His explanations, we believe in His prophecies; to us He becomes so dominatingly our Friend, that we are sure that neither life nor death nor any living creature can ever separate us from Him. That friendship, promised in our name at baptism, we have undertaken to keep unspoiled, unbroken, honoured by loyalty and constancy. So overwhelming to us can be this friendship that despite our lack of emotional pleasure in it, we are willing to forego everything that is opposed to it; to avoid persons, places and things that imperil it, so that we may aim at the height of St. Paul: 'Now I live, but not I, Christ liveth in me.'

THE SON OF GOD

I

We see then at once of what practical importance to us it is to reinforce our belief in the Divinity of Our Lord. There is sometimes a temptation to belittle the Church's exceeding care to preserve intact the very phrases of her dogmas. People grow impatient of what at times seems to them a dispute about mere words. 'What does it all matter, this squabble over an iota?' friends say to us, 'as long as you live in Christ.' Of course, it is true that Christ is more important in Himself than anything we can say about Him; but how shall we know Him unless we believe, and how shall we believe unless we are taught?

That is just where our need of Faith (i.e., of being taught and believing what we are taught) is apparent. It is true that we should live the life of Christ; but why? Because we think it beautiful? Yes; but no less because we think it true and good.

II

We are Christians because we follow Christ and believe in Him. Now when we say that we believe in Him, we mean by that at least as much as when we say we believe in doctors or politicians, viz., we think them sincere and capable in their particular science or art. We think, therefore, that Our Lord was sincere and capable as the moral Teacher of mankind, for it was as the moral and spiritual regenerator of the world that He claimed to have come. But it will not do for us to say that His teaching was very beautiful, but that, of course, He was only a good man. If He was ' only a good man ' He certainly was not even that, for He claimed to be God, the ONLY Son of God, of the same nature as the Father, His sole heir (Mark xii, 6). Not only did He use of Himself such titles as Son of God, not only did He challenge His hearers to convict Him of sin, nor ever ask the prayers of anyone, and in the Gospel of St. John make claim to great powers and knowledge, but in the parable of the Vineyard in St. Mark's Gospel, He spoke of the prophets of Israel as the servants of God, but of Himself as

THE SPACE OF LIFE BETWEEN

the ' only-begotten Son ' (using a word that occurs nowhere else in the Greek New Testament), the heir of God, the inheritor by nature of the possessions of the Father. Indeed, so angry were the Pharisees at this which seemed blasphemous to them, that they roundly accused Him to Pilate because ' He called Himself the Son of God '. That shows what they thought of what He claimed to be.

III

We have only to think for one minute to realize that no human being, no ' good man ' could possibly claim to be God, unless he were either mad, or God indeed. For the claim to be divine, made by anyone who admits that he grows tired, is thirsty or hungry, can only be accounted for by supposing that he is insane—or else that he *is really* divine. Consequently, that sharp alternative is all that is left us, when we realize that He claimed to be God. Certainly He was not ' only a good man '. He was either more than that or less, either the God He claimed to be, or else not even a good teacher to be followed. No one, however, but is struck in the Gospels by the quiet sanity He always showed and the divinity He claimed. Insane no one can call Him. What then can He have been but God ?

JESUS MOST LOVABLE

I

Our Lord communicates to us life eternal, because He is the One Mediator; and He is the One Mediator because He is God and Man. He has stooped to conquer. As God, and containing therefore the fulness of life, He has the sap whereby alone we, the branches, can live, for this sap is 'a participation in the Divine Nature' (2 Peter, i, 4); but as Man He attracts us to Himself by the beauty of His life and makes this union betwixt us and Him, even to our human imagination, also desirable and blessed. To put the problem in words, which are inaccurate and yet do more easily explain it, we can say that God's difficulty was to make our love for Him, which was in itself a duty, also a delight. Man is easily wearied of mere service, and once wearied, can hardly for long be compelled to it even through fear. Hence God's mere threats, had such been according to His Nature, would never have held man to Him for long; God's character itself, that is, God's loving understanding of us, solved the problem of man's love; so to attract men He became Man.

II

We are sociable animals. We have a keen delight in comradeship. Friendship is our need and our dominant craving. Such is the nature God gave us. When He looked at us fresh from His hands, He declared as the first thing about us that it was not good for us to be alone. Of course really we were never alone, for He was with us; but it was evident we needed not only to *have* someone with us, but to *see* that we had someone. So He created a help-mate, meet for man. That is the remedy God has always found for His creatures here. In their troubles He gives them a friend. He leads them, inspires them, consoles them by love. Consequently, when He desired that men should keep close to Him in order that His life should be shared by them, His only remedy was to come as a friend, a fellow-man, but with all the charm of outward appearance and inward character that would win their hearts to

Himself. His way to make the love of God easy was to make it a love for God-made-Man.

III

That is the secret purpose behind the Incarnation. God redeemed the world not only by dying for it (that was only one half of the work), but by getting it to live for Him. He indeed laid it down as one of the principles of life that if you want anything very much, you have in one sense to give it up altogether, to lose it in order to find it. So to find the world, He renounced it; to secure His continuance in the world, He left it; to draw its love, He let it kill Him out of hate. He knows our odd and paradoxical nature, and what queer folk we are; He knew that the only way to touch us was to let us do something dreadful against Himself. Seldom are we generous till we have been unkind; much of our goodness is inspired by occult compensation for the harm we have done by thought or word or deed. Cleverly in His Incarnation He let us put Him to death, showed us how ungrateful this was of us, and by 'an equal and necessary reaction', has caught our love for ever.

LIFE AND LOVE

I

You see the whole of religion can be compressed into these two words which are so frequently on Our Lord's lips in the Gospel of St. John. Try to remember the numberless texts that include one or other of these words, or even both of them, and you will be astonished to find with what frequency they occur in those great passages of the New Testament that have always moved you. And why not indeed? There is nothing else so desirable here or anywhere as those two things, life and love. Life is a condition of all enjoyment and love is a condition, in its turn, for all real life. You cannot separate these two that God has put together. Life drives us to love, and love deepens life. Love demands life, is stronger even than life's rival, death, is stronger even than its own rival, hate, it is a fierce and consuming power, more terrible than an army set in battle array, more terrible than war which feeds on death, a 'Lord of terrible aspect'.

II

We think of love then as something which for all its attractiveness and unifying power, has nothing to do with dalliance or mere weakness. Sometimes love may find us in a maudlin mood, and then selfishness may creep in; but love itself is a passion, a thing rather of violence than of weakness. What dreadful crimes has it not, in one form or another, driven men to commit, because it is violent and unruly? Life, too, is a violent thing: it courses through one's veins, it stirs, thrills, impels, uplifts a man. It expresses itself in motion. It cannot keep still. Howsoever rhythmic it may be in sleep and unconsciousness, it is never wholly quiet; death is very still, hushed, silent. Life is awake and about and always stirring. Dignity and reserved strength move us just because we can see the sign of strain and guess the pent force that is being held up, and contrast in a swift act of imagination what appears with that which lies behind appearance. The silence of life is tense and awful, because incredibly and actively protected by a barricade of power against the urgent pressure and clatter of noise and cries.

III

It would be very foolish then to think that religion, which is the knowledge and love of God, can be a boring thing if it is really concerned with life and love. My religion may bore me, but that can only be because it is not religion at all. It may have the outward forms of religion in perfect order. It may be intellectually an orthodoxy without fear and without reproach: it may have the actual controls of true religion, but it has quite evidently missed the inner heart and meaning of it. What's the test of a man's religion? There are two tests: love and life. Is my religion a stirring thing, not emotionally, indeed, but vitally? Does it move me to live better, more fully, more richly? And does it drive me to love? Puritanism may be called religion, just as revivalism is called religion. Neither of them is religion at all. They are semi-religions. Revivalism breeds immorality and puritanism breeds cruelty, whereas what Our Master came to give us was life and love, a noble life expressed in the love of God and Man.

SOURCES OF LIFE

I

Why do I find religion sometimes—often, perhaps—very dull and heavy? Only because I have not a love of God. Yes, but that is no answer at all; it merely shifts the question further back and leaves us where we were, for we have only to put to ourselves the same question in a new form: why have I not a love of God, to see that the answer was no answer. We do not want religion to be a bore; we should very much like it to be interesting, particularly if it is possible to combine religion (that is, a love of God) with the happy and pleasant things which are in life and which, after all, were put there by God Himself presumably for our enjoyment. Here we get to the heart of our real problem, namely, how am I to make the love of God something more than a mere form? Boredom can only come into religion when that religion is merely formal—a great danger, because religion tends of itself by routine to become formal. Can I keep it fresh and fragrant? Cannot I put lavender in the drawer with it to preserve this freshness of fragrance in it when I lay it aside after each act of prayer?

II

Does this simile help you to see the remedy? It is not that religion needs lavender. It is that it must never be laid aside. We can vary the metaphor and say that, like a man's muscle, it needs use to keep it fresh and fit. Religion is not like your clothes which you can put off. It is not even like your skin. It is deeper than these external things, deeper than beauty. It is under the skin. Religion does not become conspicuous by being absent. It becomes conspicuous only by constant presence, by repeated action, by daily, hourly, unceasing repetition. There is no end to it, just because it is alive: 'I am the Way and the Truth and the Life' (John xiv, 6). Truth, faith, religion, are alive or not at all. Only repeated acts of religion and of faith, can keep them alive; and by repeated acts of religion, something more is meant than regularity in prayer or the sacraments. Religion implies this, but no less it implies taking a high and noble view of life. It means aiming at kindness in conversation and act, having ideals of generosity and keeping to them, laying aside suspicion and cynicism, 'believing all things, hoping all things, enduring all things' (1 Cor., xiii, 7). A difficult task? Good heavens, yes; the most difficult of all. But then He called His service a Cross when He first told us of it, a burden and a yoke.

III

Is it possible to keep my ideals unsullied, and still go on believing in man in spite of experience? Yes, it is possible: first, by a constant reading of the Gospels and by trying to recall the splendid phrases in which are flung at us the tremendous and perilous principles of Christ, 'The Kingdom of God and His Justice' (Matt. vi, 33). Secondly, by endeavouring to live up to our love of our neighbour, whoever he be or whatever he may do. To Christ Who saw truly, the publican and sinners were better folk than the Pharisees; but *we* cannot judge any man. We must take all into our sympathy. Thirdly, by basing ourselves on the sacramental food of the Eucharist, which means eternal life springing up in us and breaking out into life and love. 'The blood, that is the life,' is given us there. There we can come, if we will, into such close relationship with Him, that we are fired by His enthusiasms and find religion a devouring flame.

INDIVIDUALITY

I

ALL through our school days, and even earlier, we looked forward to our leaving school as the date of our emancipation. We should then, at last, we thought, be free. We were perfectly right. Up till then, we had been ' under tutors and governors ', who ruled us and our day: thence forward we could be masters of ourselves. And this is a very great step indeed, for the only thing we really can have here on earth is freedom. Everything is provided for us, but freedom, i.e., the being our own masters, is entirely our own doing; God has made all things else obey Him blindly, but we are free; our service must be a free service, an affair of choice, deliberate, with the will in it. Moreover, it must be the free offering of ourselves, the real self that God wanted us to be. A mother sits and dreams the future of her baby boy sleeping upstairs, picturing in the firelight or out in the garden the career she plots and plans for him. God, too, has His purposes for the child.

II

Because, then, we are free to be ourselves, we have, each one of us to be what God wanted us to be. Now God is prudent, does no superfluous thing, and therefore, in making each one of us different, meant us to remain so, with an individuality of our own. We have each, then, to be ourselves. But what do we find? No sooner have we emerged from school and have acquired our longed-for freedom, than everything, within and without, conspires against this freedom. First there is the heavy pressure of convention. Naturally, we must be ruled to some extent by convention, for it is often no more than crystallized politeness; it saves time, it saves us from bothering over our choice in little things. We accept the shapes and fashions of our age. That is all very right and proper. But we can easily get into a frame of mind, which hates to have to judge for itself, make its own choice and leave the common run of men. Conventional judgements, conventional standards of popularity or fashions, these crush all personality and turn men and boys into parrots or gramophones, are far more tyrannous than any 'tutor or governor', and more insidious. People who belaud freedom are often not free at all, are merely repeating phrases, content to be in their lives like anyone else.

III

Again, things within conspire against our freedom, namely our passions and bad habits: 'Whosoever committeth sin is the servant of sin'. We know that from experience as well as from Scripture. We want to break from our habits of evil, we try, we fail—we, if you please, who talk of our independence, freedom, manly dignity, and the rest of it. Sin, then, breaks in on our freedom, and prevents us from being masters of ourselves. What has emancipation from school done for us, who are at the mercy of forces within and without? We have no escape but One; He shall lead us Who is truth: 'the truth shall make you free'. There is no freedom comparable with freedom built on truth. Judge true judgements. Hold to your ideas if they be of divine giving. Do not be afraid of having your own point of view. Be very humble, but always truthful, and convention will not destroy you, nor by God's grace will sin hold you captive long. But you must work hard to protect your individuality if you wish to be free.

OUR CALLING

I

WE based our individuality upon our individual creation by God. We believe that God made us, our bodies through the ministration of others, but our souls directly Himself. These souls, then, were severally created by God, and therefore each of them for a separate purpose. Since He made us individually and distinctly, He made us for some purpose of His own. Moreover, because He made us for a purpose, He must, out of fairness to Himself as well as to us have given us all the qualities necessary for carrying out that purpose. It were foolish to act otherwise, to make us for some job and not give us the means to complete it. Hence we can argue from the very nature of God, His wisdom, His justice, His power, that we each have something to do for Him in this life, and that He has taken care to make us capable of doing it; and when we say that we have something to do for Him, we are not merely referring to prayers and pious exercises, but to a complete life.

II

Now that is our calling and our vocation, namely, God's purpose, the career for which He has fitted us. It must be of great importance for us to find out what this career is, not only because it is God's will, but because it is the supreme thing for us, that which alone we shall succeed in doing properly. Nothing is at its best unless it is being used for the purpose for which it was intended; the blade of a knife may turn a screw, but a screw-driver is better for the purpose; a sword may be used as a ploughshare but it is more satisfactory as a sword. Consequently we are only likely to be at our best when we have found the calling God created us for and gifted us purposely to achieve. But how am I to discover what precisely He did intend me for? There are, after all, a number of vocations at which I am likely to do equally well or equally badly. Sometimes we are drawn in one direction, sometimes in another. Which really is God's? Which is my one calling that alone will be fully successful?

Prayer for light to find it certainly will help me, advice of others will guide me, natural instinct will incline me in a certain direction, family traditions, etc. But I want some sign. The only real signs are my talents. 'Tinker, tailor, soldier, sailor, ploughboy, apothecary . . .' so the old rhyme runs on. Which of these is mine? What is the principle by which alone I can settle? It is this. I must take as my vocation that career in which my gifts, talents, qualifications, such as I judge them to be, can be put to their fullest possible use.

III

First, then, I have to tabulate on paper what I am good at; secondly, I set down the various professions open to me; thirdly, I must make up my mind for which of them my talents best fit me. How shall I know my talents? Others can tell me, and my own experience and my inclinations, for chiefly (though not always) we like the things we are good at. But perhaps when I have done all this I am really not sure what I am to be? Must I be sure? No, for we are none of us infallible, and may easily make mistakes. A mistake on our part will not disturb God. All He wants to see is that we are trying to find out His will. He certainly wants us to do His will, and will therefore be making it plain to us, and if we miss it through our stupidity and not because we have not tried, then, He can have no fault to find with us: ' God doth not ask a perfect work, but infinite desire '.

THE PRIESTHOOD

I

An easy example of choosing a vocation is to take the priesthood. It is a very practical example, because nearly every Catholic boy or young man, whether Catholic by inheritance or a convert, puts to himself the idea of the priesthood or the religious life, to see whether he is meant for it or not. Sometimes he hopes he has a vocation for it, sometimes only he is afraid lest he may have one. How is he to determine the matter for himself? Prayer, naturally, must be the beginning and the end of it. It begins it by his asking God to give him light to see; it ends it by his asking for the courage to do. When the time comes then for him to make up his mind he devotes himself very specially to prayer. Further, he seeks advice from those who best know him, his parents, masters, friends, the priest to whom he has usually gone to confession. They can help him by telling him what their impression is from the little or the great deal they have seen of him.

II

Prayer, then, and advice, are of assistance. Then he has to face for himself in the quietness of a retreat, or with such detachment as his surroundings allow, the decision as far as he is concerned. Later, other people will have a say in settling his vocation if he does decide to go on for the priesthood, but it is his part now. How is he, then, to settle it? First, what has he to settle? He has to settle whether God has intended him for a priest. There are, therefore, two things that he must be perfectly clear about before he can settle this: he must be clear in his own mind as to what a priest should be, and also as to what sort of person he is himself. Settling a vocation is (*a*) sizing up yourself, and (*b*) sizing up the profession you think you may be intended to adopt. What, then, is a priest? He is one who stands between God and man, to give to God the things of man, and to man the things of God. Consequently he has to be interested both in God and in man. He will be no use as a priest if he be fastidious or difficult to get on with, or unpunctual in his habits

THE SPACE OF LIFE BETWEEN

and temperament: at least, if he be any of these in an overwhelming degree. Again, he must not be wedded to mere external things, he must have an interest in divine things, in God and His life, His Kingdom, His beauty, goodness, justice, truth. These are what alone will concern him later on if he is a priest. Can he face a life in which comforts will not come his way, where he will be at the beck and call of others, where he will never really be 'off duty' till he dies, where he will never have the fostering comfort or the devoted love of a woman?

III

To be sure of all this he has to know himself. Is he a sociable fellow?

For a religious life he must be even more sociable than for the secular priesthood.

Can he 'rough it' not merely in food and house and bed, but by having perhaps no one of his own social standing to talk to? Has he the power to make a rule and keep it? Can he live a life that is really more at the service of others than of himself? Of course, it would be absurd to suppose that such a life as this were possible to human nature alone. It needs necessarily the support, inspiration, grace of God. But God's grace perfects nature and does not destroy it. We have no business to ask for miracles. We must go as we are led, not indeed perfect before we join, but attracted and not repelled by these things.

MY CAREER

I

OTHER professions, other forms of life, lie before those who know that the priestly life is not for them. The ways of God's service are as manifold as there are men to serve Him. Each has to reach God by his own mountain-path, clambering upwards to that great height. Yet it is not really a path left to his choosing, but the path God has cleared for him. God has a way cut for each man; each man has the adventure of finding it; a real adventure, for though the light be good, his eyes fail him or, it may be, the road winds a great deal, and not very much is evident or clear. Much patience and carefulness are needed by him. Not at the first glance shall he see his way clear before him. He must just wait patiently, for time will show it to him when it is due. Time is an ally of ours in our quest and not,

THE SPACE OF LIFE BETWEEN

for all its seeming delay, an obstacle. After all, then, even though God has cut and cleared the path, there is always an adventure in discovering it, not because it is not clearly marked, but because we so blindly have to grope our way.

II

These other careers then (once we have chosen that for which our God-given talents best fit us) demand from us in their turn a definite preparation. No more than the priesthood can they be entered on lightly. They are sacred, each one of them, for they are divinely purposed: 'What God hath made let no man call common or unclean'. 'Soldier, sailor, tinker, tailor', for all their homely sound, demand yet a life-work from a son of God. The avenue to them is no less sacred. We would think ill of the student of the priesthood who neglected the studies of his sacred calling, partly because we hold his office to be sacred, partly because, if he be not properly prepared for his ministry, he will not be able to help those who come to him in distress: 'The hungry sheep look up and are not fed'. He imperils not his soul only, but theirs also by his negligence. All this would be equally true of every career; the doctor, evidently, who has idled as a medical student, will, through his ignorance, cause pain and death that lie to the charge of his soul; the lawyer will be bound to restitution where his culpable ignorance, through neglected studies, has lost his client's case; the soldier and the sailor who have slacked or never properly learnt their trade, the merchant, the very dustmen and road-cleaners, have not merely a sacred calling that needs preparation, whether little or great, but by their remissness must one day imperil others whom it was their duty to have served and saved. I have to realize, then, the high responsibility of my profession.

III

In these trades, then, there is only one way of action if the world is to be rescued from its distress, and that is by honest work. Yet we cannot help noticing that schools are often more concentrated on making records of their games and scholarships than on the steady work of the normal boy. Again, later the technical study years of a profession are ruled by a convention that makes it 'bad form' for the individual to be keenly devoted to his work. The name of 'swot' or its corresponding, though more dignified, synonyms, is considered an insult: whereas it is the duty of each of us, according to the measure of our talents, to labour to the best of our power at the career to which we are called, and at the skilled preparation that such a career demands. Nor is this selfishness. It is due to our reverence for God and for the carrying out of His will; it is due to the dependence of our neighbour on us, due to our love of country, to that self-respect without which our manhood cannot be upheld.

SELF-INDULGENCE

I

NATURALLY, all through life our great enemy is our own selfishness. Howsoever we determine our spiritual life, howsoever even we determine our temporal life, our main obstacle to proving our worth, capacity, ideals, is just ourselves: 'the things which come out from a man, they defile a man'. It is not so much that which comes against us from without as the traitor within our gates that is the cause of our defeats. It is our selfishness, our self-indulgence, that is responsible for most of our failures. Nor can our self-indulgence be narrowed down to any one particular form of evil, for it will appear differently to each of us, tricked out in the disguise most alluring to each soul. For obviously self-indulgence is only ourselves masquerading under the appearance of something else, some sport, or pleasure or hobby; and consequently the evil of it will lie not in the thing itself but in the time or expense or immoderation that it demands of us.

II

To some folk cards are a very great temptation. Why a temptation? Is it not prejudice that makes us speak of them as evil things? Surely there is no harm in cards? Of course there is none. Cards were invented to please a mad king, but they have been developed to interest intelligent people. A game of cards can be as instructive and as useful for training the mind as a game of chess: only, we must confess, people do not play cards to be instructed or trained. Why should they, indeed? All the rest of their day ought to be occupied with work; the evenings then can be devoted to recreation or the afternoons to bridge parties. Nor need there be any harm at all even in those card games which depend entirely or almost entirely for their playing, upon chance. Indeed sheer luck is more absorbing to the average player than mere skill, because in such games he feels a greater sense of equality among all the players: there is a chance for everyone, and the chances are nearly the same for everyone. To be defeated by others repeatedly even in a game discourages you from continuing it, but to lose repeatedly in a game of chance does not discourage you from going on with it, for you feel that every defeat only increases the odds in favour of your winning at the next throw. That is the whole lure of gambling. If you have won, you think at once that you are in luck, and therefore of your greater possibility of winning more; if you have lost, you are sure that your luck will turn, and with every loss you cling to that hope only more determinedly.

III

Not wrong in themselves; games of cards, whether of skill or chance, have yet in them an element of danger. To most people whom cards do not bore, they are perilous. They absorb time and money and provoke an unhealthy excitement. Time and money may indeed be devoted to them without harm, so long as they can be afforded; but either of these may easily be squandered beyond our means. Certainly to play endlessly with people older than ourselves is dangerous, because of the loss of our time and money. Those older than we are, presumably have more free time and certainly more money than we, and can play for higher stakes. Yet we have too much pride, probably rightly, not to agree to play at their level, a level that is compatible with their pockets but not with ours. In club and mess, beware of the older gamester, not because he is necessarily dishonest, but because he has usually more money to spend than you. Yet when all has been said against it, there is no game so handy, so companionable, so recreative, so exciting, within so simple a compass as a hand of cards.

WOMEN

I

After God, according to the inspired account in the Old Testament, had created man and set him in the midst of the wonderful Garden of Eden, He said: 'It is not good for man to be alone: let us make him a help like unto himself'. In that graphic story with which we are confronted at the beginning of the Scriptures, we find that it was the loneliness of man which pierced the heart of God, a loneliness evident in a world that as yet brought forth no thorns or thistles, and needed no labour or toil to bring its crops and fruits to fruition. Even in such happy surroundings man's loneliness was apparent: to remedy it God sent him a 'help'. Then when the disaster of the Fall had come to pass, and the two were to be driven out from 'the paradise of pleasure', Adam called the name of his wife Eve because she was 'the mother of all living'. She had been the sharer of his joyous life; she was to be the sharer of his burdens, in her double office of wife and mother. She was to be even something more: she was to inspire him, point the more excellent way, 'under her husband's power', yet 'the mother of all living'.

II

In God's design, therefore, woman was to be a help to man. Yet from the start it would seem that she has failed him, for we are taught that she has led him astray: since then, too, it would seem that she has been responsible for much evil in man—at least in the sense that she has caused (as purpose, motive, goal) so much of his deeds of passion. That is not really true. It is man who has been his own undoing; in his passionate acts of cruelty, of crime, of greed, it is not the woman whom he has sought: it is merely himself. He may consider that other and not himself to be blameworthy ('she gave me to eat'); whereas in these crimes it is precisely the others whom he is in pursuit of for his own ends whom he outrages or ignores. It is but another proof of his foolish self-deceit for man to blame his partner or helpmate or love for his sins and blunders. It is himself whom he has to blame; for women were meant to help him to achieve a good which without them he could not in his loneliness otherwise attain. Love was intended to be the pillar of fire that should lead him across his wilderness, for love carries a man beyond himself. His first impulse under its influence is one of joy and rapture, but his second, following quickly on its heels, is one of humility. He knows his own unworthiness of that which has been given him. He can hardly believe in his good fortune, is afraid lest because of his unworthiness his love will not be returned, or shown at least only out of pity or as a passing whim; certainly he does not expect to find his own full love equalled.

III

Now the dangers of this love are two-fold: (*a*) when the sense of unworthiness, of humility, has lifted and disappeared, there is the old peril of passion coming back again: and passion begins in thoughts and imaginations that have not been guarded or controlled. Love must quench passion by insisting upon the due reverence for the beloved: ' Who so profaneth the temple of God, him shall God destroy '. Each body is a living temple of God's Holy Spirit. The other danger (*b*) is inconstancy, due in the main to a man's giving himself at once and too easily to the first object that pleases. He will soon tire. He should think, then, rather of the one who attracts him than of himself; for her sake he should give himself only when he is sure of himself and sure that there will be no danger of inconstancy. The ' first love ', for all its humorous exaggeration and its ' plentiful lack ' of humour, may indeed be the freshest, the most fragrant, the most lasting of all; a man may find at once a help like unto himself. But he should remember that love is not true love if it be selfish. His love for women should raise him, not drag him down.

LOVE

I

Love, then, was given man by God to be of help to him. Without it, he would have found himself alone in a state which God judged to be 'not good'; and we can see how love becomes such a help, for it lifts a man above his own selfishness and fires him with an ideal which endows his work and sufferings with a new purpose, makes them of value and gives a centre to them all. Love, therefore, is the great power that God set in the world to move and to establish man. It moves him, bringing him forward, giving a motive for his ambition that will rob his strongest efforts of selfishness; just when he is of age to meet the work of his life, and before he has scrambled past its period of drudgery, when the first interest has worn off and before he has settled down to the real skilled labour of his career, midway between the wayward vitalities of boyhood and the serious yet increasing interests of his responsible years, he has love to drive him: yet it does more than drive, for it settles him in his career. He cannot afford to throw up his way of livelihood, because in front of him lies the life of love, wherein others will be dependent on him. His risks now are not his alone; and whatever a man might rightly dare for himself, he cannot risk for others.

II

Love, therefore, must be considered in its practical results if its place in life is to be fully recognized and used. Nevertheless, it is chiefly its romantic side that is thought of, and here we meet at once with the humours of literature. The love episode has its comic reliefs in drama and literature. Indeed, the comic element in it, its incongruous ecstasy, its empty and vain repetitions, its over-sugared phrases of impossible perfections, have overflowed from books and the stage into life. By their elders children are jokingly paired together as sweethearts, and laughed at. The youngster still at school is chaffed over his infatuations: the girl is jestingly accused of her long line of captives. Probably this is quite sane and healthy. It certainly forms one staple element in the humorous press which represent the middle-class prejudices of the English people. But there is a danger also in this belittling, this endless guffaw, that greets on the stage and in life the opening drama of love. Granted that it needs being laughed at from time to time, has it not at present need rather for respect?

III

The romantic side of love is now at a discount. The lengthening list of divorce cases proves that over and over again. That love should really be stronger than hate, that for richer and poorer, for better and worse, love should hold its worshippers together against every weakness of human nature, seems now to be thought impossible. 'I no longer love you' is the burden of the letter read in the divorce court, written by one to the other to show that the end of their companionship has come; as though love were a thing beyond one's control, and once having begun can die down all by itself, without either party being able to prevent it. This is not true, need not be true. Love can be kept alive. Yet love is romantic, and to save it, its romance must be kept alive. It is not mere emotion, for it must outlast the emotions, it must be supported by every truth and ever dogma, it must be nourished upon reverence, it must be realized to be the state wherein men and women are at their finest and best. Cleansed of untruth and selfishness and yet robbed of none of its beauty, it must be recognized to be the only genuine human force than can give man vitality and virtue, steadiness, courage, enduring hope, and a remedy against passion for the men and women of the world.

MARRIAGE

I

MARRIAGE is a divine institution carrying divine grace. It is love come to its normal result; itself, however, a mere episode in the development of love. For marriage is not only a sacrament, it is the beginning of a new life. The sacrament marks a new stage in the life of love; henceforth the need for love will be greater, not less, its purposes finer, its expression more noble. Love-making perhaps precedes marriage, but the love so made must endure past the moment when the sacrament is accomplished: indeed, now a divine flame is added to the fire of love, a constancy given it to keep it always alight, unquenchable. It must be recognized, therefore, that the business of the sacrament is to add a divine steadfastness to what might become fickle. The words of the ceremony imply that above all

all else: 'For better, for worse, till death do us part'. Hence the indissoluble nature of the marriage-tie is evident from the purpose of the sacrament itself, and is referred to by the very wording of its form.

II

But the graces of marriage are not merely to support the human love with a divine assurance, to make perpetual its patience, understanding, sympathy, unselfishness, constancy; they are also to help towards the carrying out of the purposes of the human union, the responsibilities of fatherhood and motherhood. Pleasure divorced from the responsibilities that alone make it lawful, is the most demoralizing of forces. It cannot but degrade and debase, for of itself it would become sheer selfishness. Hence it will always follow that any stage of civilization that legalizes divorce will simultaneously begin to control the birthrate: the two movements always tend to co-exist. Birth-control leads to divorce, as divorce to birth-control. They are the symptoms of the same disease, a pleasure-loving, excitement-seeking, workless society. Birth-control and divorce are invariable concomitants in the life of a nation that has surrendered its ideal of work or service to an ideal of pleasure and wealth. Is, then, all birth-control forbidden? May one do nothing to control procreation? Certainly a man and woman may determine for some grave reason that they should limit the number of their children. But the reason must be really grave and really actual, not a mere surmise. Under these conditions, how may birth be lawfully controlled? By abstention. By no other means? By no other direct means. No one is allowed by Catholic teaching to do anything that directly and of itself gives the pleasure of the marriage-act and yet frustrates directly and positively the end and justification of it.

III

With ideals so absolute and at times so hard to flesh and blood steadily before a man's eyes, he will be careful of the choice of his partner in life. It is for this that mixed marriages, as they are called, sometimes turn out ill. The non-Catholic wife, on whom will come the pains of child-bearing, may find it hard to understand the teaching of the faith and see no reason for being bound by it. Yet as a wife she can have no choice but to submit. Again, it is here that hasty marriages may turn out ill: on the stern Catholic principles of an enduring love and the duties of fatherhood. It is, then, with the vision of motherhood-to-be of the wife of his choice that a man must determine his help-mate. Not only her present gifts, but those she will one day need, must be considered before he asks her to share the strong ruling of the Church. Can man so control and steady his love? Rather, love itself, controlled and cleanly, as it needs must be, will makes its own unerring choice almost without deliberation, but with a swift insight that only seems indeliberate because of this past unselfish chastity that has prepared it for this hour.

FRIENDSHIP

I

WHAT difference is there between love and friendship? It is hard to determine, perhaps, with any absolute exactness. To Shelley, the word friendship had a meaning of greater unselfishness than love. Friendship was less passionate than love, and implied that a man gave more of himself and received less in return. Perhaps more usually a man's friends are thought of as of his own sex. If this be so then in spite of Shelley's distinction, the friendships of boyhood, school friendships, can be passionate enough and hard to distinguish from what Shelley has called love. It is written that the friendship of David for Jonathan was 'passing the love of women'. We can take it, therefore, as a fact that the friendships that a man makes with his friends of schooldays or of later life, may be as passionate as any others. In the artificial surroundings of school and its necessary isolation from home interests, the spontaneous affection of a boy finds no outlet other than the other boys; if he be of affectionate nature, he will turn passionately to his friends. Partly, therefore, by his mere circumstances, a boy is drawn into mysterious and ardent friendships with other boys. This may be perilous: let us admit, however, that it is certainly inevitable.

II

Now when school-days are done, this friendship does not always cease, for there are natures that by some turn of temperament are drawn more easily to appreciate, admire, and love their own sex than the other. This may lead to sin in the same way as other loves may do; but it is not necessarily evil. It is a trick of temperament, which may have a psychological origin. Certainly it cannot safely be ignored. Everywhere, in every stage of culture, under every climate and in every condition, the thing has always been; not, indeed in the majority of cases, but in a large and eager minority. Let us at least recognize that it cannot well be helped, that there is no reason why it should be prevented. It is of absolute necessity if the matter is to be dealt with at all honestly, that I should recognize these tendencies and facts, and recognize them to be in themselves perfectly innocent: 'Each is drawn by native preference'. This preference for men by a man is then, of its own nature, innocent, and need contain no evil; but it is not innocent, necessarily, and may become as desolating, debasing, and destructive, as any other power or talent worked to an unmeasured extent. A man who falls in love with every girl, who seeks and pursues whatever pleases his eye, is no better and no worse off than he who pursues as selfishly those of his own sex who attract and appeal to him: uncontrolled emotions are degrading in every direction and for whatever purpose. There are not the same consequences in each excess, but the consequences of each are terrible.

III

The friendships that we have with others of our own sex may be as valuable to us as those we speak of usually as our loves. They can possess us as wholly, can give us as high a measure of unselfishness, can form as great a joy. But friendship, no less than love, has its rubrics, conditions, and limitations. It must be entered into deliberately and with eyes wide open to the consequence. A friend, like a lover, is for all time: ' That is not love which alters when it alteration finds and bends with the removers to remove '. I must choose warily, for I choose for always. Again, with friendship as with love, with loss of reverence comes friendship's own ruin, for respect is the basis of the enduring equalities of love; so that passion beyond control, a blundering, vulgar thing, which destroys the freshness and fragrance of affection, destroys friendship as completely as it does love. Friendship is a great gift, if we remember that it is carried in an earthen vessel, delicate, 'a seldom pleasure', and is only to be kept from evil by the thought of Our Lord present as a third in it. Thereby it becomes full of unselfishness and sacrifice. It may become evil, it is not necessarily an evil, it may be a great good.

WINE

I

Amongst all peoples love and wine have been for good and ill, in defence and in denunciation, bracketed together. Everywhere the vine has woven its tendrils round the statue of beauty in the vineyards of Engaddi '; for both from one and the other man has gained a sense of rapture that lifts him out of the level of his normal days. Early in the history of tribes wine is always a sacred thing, proper to the altar, making man frenzied and somehow divine, so that a thrill beyond the reach of ordinary experience passes through him and sets in him the stir and wonder of a life wider, ampler, more free, than the life he is familiar with. In mythology it is the gift of a God, who suffers sometimes the same fate as that other friend of man, Prometheus, who first gave him fire. Yet the vine, they thought, for all its beauty of form and colour, was of the earth, drawing from the earth its life, and helplessly dependent on the earth for its existence, its growth, and continuance. The bewildered mind of man seeing no proportion between the soil whence the vine sprang and the airy unsubstantial dreams to which it gave birth, sought for a more imaginative origin for it and seemed to find that only a heavenly source was adequate to explain its effects.

II

But while to the primitive mind and to the mind of the poet, wine was sacred, heaven-brought, to the less ignorant and less visionary it was merely ribald and amusing in its effects. The man staggering under the mood of its excess, with pugnacity or helplessness, with his mixed eagerness and lethargy, presented chiefly its comic side. He was so ineffectual in all he aimed at, in all he strove to be; lurched so unevenly when he most needed steadiness, that the sharp incongruities between his efforts and their lack of attainment, between his words and their ideas, between his words and their pronunciation, caused an irresistible impulse to laugh. The comic element is so obvious, so droll, and so evidently unintentional, that the sight of drunkenness produces roars of laughter.

For all its beastliness, its most dominant impression on the beholder of it is its appeal to his sense of humour.

III

How strange a thing! To excite laughter and derision by showing man as low as any of the brute creation (lower, in fact, since the greater height from which he falls is obvious in the comparison), and yet to lift him to conditions wherein he seems more neighbourly to the gods, to render him ineffectual and yet endow him with ampler dreams, to pitch him into incongruities and yet to rescue him from his dull normal dreariness. What strange thing is this that man has made, his plaything yet his tyrant, the child of his invention, but at times the master of his will. Well, there you have the paradox of wine. It is no real solution of the problem of intoxication to prohibit drink altogether; you may, by law, defer its use for a while, or hold it over, or keep it back till man is likely to be more impartial in his judgements of it. But can one do more ? It is at best a temporary expedient. It must fail. The problem has to be solved really by each individual for himself. Temperance is essentially a measure that for its effectiveness must be settled by me for myself.

Like love, like gambling, like the other passions that are tangled with the roots of man's nature, the thirst for an intoxicant has a purpose, but that purpose is subservient to man's destiny. Normally, it has only to be controlled. Abnormally, it may have to be renounced. How far is it needed by me? How far does it hinder me? No one can tell but the man himself. Certainly, drunkenness is beastly, despite its comic appearance. We must avoid it ourselves. We must never instigate another to drunkenness, as though it were a practical joke or a mere lark. We may not, however, forbid intoxicating drink to those who find it a help towards work and life, or even a source of harmless joy.

PURITY

I

IT is clear that all the time in these last meditations we have been on the edge of a subject which in a way controls or tests them all. In love and friendship and marriage, in wine even, the thing menaced is chiefly purity, or perhaps more accurately, we may say that what best guards a man in them all is cleanness of heart. It is sometimes thought that when purity is praised it is some physical virtue that is being extolled. This is partly true, for purity is indeed a virtue not of thought only, but of action as well; but certainly it would be mischievous to suppose that the mere physical side of it would suffice. We preach no crusade in favour of mere abstention from evil; we seek rather to establish in our minds and imaginations a perception of a great ideal, not negatively refraining from evil deeds, but positively establishing a definite type of good. I have to realize that when I have avoided evil actions or evil words or thoughts, I have only begun to understand what Our Lord came to teach.

II

What did Our Lord lay down for us, His followers? He began by laying down first, that love was the fulfilling of the law. We have to love God and our neighbour for God's sake, and we have to love ourselves. Love should be the principle of all human acts, as it is the principle of the acts of God. Secondly, Our Lord showed what He meant by love of the brotherhood, by asserting for example in many parables the doctrine of forgiveness even to the extent of death. We must love by forgiving, by not requiting evil with evil, by continuing our dutiful service in spite of the hostile spirit with which our kindness may be met. Love, then, which is the motive of our acts, is essentially an act of unselfishness. Further, this unselfish love is controlled and orderly, because in whatever circumstances it finds itself, it seeks never itself, but the good of the object of its love. Love gives, but does not seek to get. It does indeed receive benefits, and it knows they will come, it is fed and strengthened by them; but it is not dependent on them, and does not seek them out. Love, then, though it be self-satisfying, nevertheless, forgets self: 'Blessed are the clean of heart for they shall see God'. This vision of God is not merely a reward, it is also a consequence. Those whose hearts are clean are those precisely who have seen God in their loved ones, in their friendships; and in virtue of that vision have acted and lived. Their friendships are precisely what they are because they have realized them to be the result of a divine choice.

III

The sacredness of love, that it comes because of a sympathy divinely established between me and my friend, is the best protection or guarantee which I have for its endurance. But it is no less the protection of its purity. Cleanness, therefore, of heart, means no loss of power, no dissipation of interests, no unrestrained, and therefore weakened emotions; it is virile, positive, based on a personal perception of the divine safeguards of human love. Consequently, it is itself best ensured by the remembrance that Our Lord set it as the aim of life: at Communion, at Mass, we have to find our real source of purity. It must grow out of affection for

Our Lord. Impurity means that we are by nature affectionate, but that this power of affection is squandered, disorderly. We can only get the better of this unruliness not by fighting it, but by plighting our troth with Him. Once we have re-established our personal friendship with Him, and in Communion been made one with Him, we shall be able to look on our friends through His eyes. We shall love them more and not less than before, indeed, it is they whom we shall love and seek, and not ourselves. Love of God alone can dry up love of self, as love for Christ could alone cure the malady of the Magdalen.

OUR LADY

I

To her clients, Our Lady has stood, above all her other glories, as representing and inspiring the virtue of purity. Whatever claims she has to our reverence, the claim of her purity has probably been more obvious to Christians than any other, more compelling, more effective, more popular. Note, for example, what Catholic dogma has to say about her. The first thing that Catholic dogma says is that she was conceived immaculate. What does that mean ? It means that what happens to us at Baptism happened to her at the moment of her conception through the foreseen merits of the Redeemer Who was to be her son. Not only, however, was she preserved beforehand from that sin from which we afterwards are cleansed, but she was also prevented by God's grace from suffering the evil results of it.

She was saved from the least defilement of original sin and from the spiritual effects of it, whereas we have gradually through life to try to get ourselves absolutely under control. A saint is one who, through heroic love of God, reaches a high level of this self-mastery. Where the saints end, Our Lady began. God gave her to start with, what He gives to others only as the fruit of a hard war with temptation painfully sustained and loyally persevered in.

II

The Angel saluted her as 'full of grace', and that before she had received the special graces of her motherhood. Before the offer had been put to her and been accepted, an angel had bowed to her in reverence, as already greater than himself; then he set before her on God's behalf the great choice; her acceptance was made in the perfect language of humility, and 'in her eyes there shone the light of motherhood'. From that moment an increase of grace came to her to fit her for her new office. At once God lay in her womb, was forming for Himself from her flesh and blood the material for the body of Christ, and surely took charge of her that she should be as worthy of her high prerogative as it was possible for mortal to be. It does not seem fantastic to suppose that God gives to each the graces and helps needed for his work in life, that those whom He calls to higher vocations have the greater needs, that those who are to be nearer to His person should also be fitted for their nearness by especial preparatory graces. If each soul has the grace required for its state of life, what must have been the graces given to her who was to be the Mother of Christ?

III

We affirm, therefore, as Catholics, that the graces given to Our Lady (given, remember) were the highest graces given to any redeemed human being. Angels bowed to her, Prophets foretold her coming, Apostles were put in her charge as their Mother. She was full of grace before her Child was conceived, and she steadily grew in grace by corresponding to what had been given her; blessed indeed as His Mother, more blessed because she heard His word and kept it. God spoke to her incessantly and she heard and obeyed. Because, therefore, she was preserved from sin and had been saved from the disastrous dissipation of powers that follows on original sin, she was able to make use of every opportunity of increasing her love of God. Her mental gifts were untainted, unflawed; she could concentrate wholly and without distraction on whatever she did. Nothing led her off from the object that the will set before her mind. She was alert and wholehearted in all she did, because the fatal consequences of original sin under which we suffer, troubled her not at all. Think, then, of her as of one who was made at her beginning what the saints are in their ending, who from the height at which they finish began her climb; then you will realize how wonderful she is, and how the thought of her greatness has filled the mind of the Church.

TOWER OF IVORY

I

Our lady's wonderful holiness was different in degree from the holiness of the saints, but not in kind, for holiness is always the same: it means a great love of God. With the steady increase of grace came also, and naturally, an increase in the love of God, for the two are the same. Consequently we have to think of her as ever increasing her love of God with each fresh impulse of grace. Free from sin as she was from the moment of her conception, that the flesh and blood of her Son might spring from an unstained womb, she began her conscious life with a love for God. Then as each event befell her in the marvellous pageant of the Incarnation, it meant a succession of higher grace to fit her for the advancing demands to be made on her, and, therefore, more love of God; the annunciation and her stirrings of motherhood, the birth of the Child, His epiphany to the Gentiles, the growing years of boyhood, the loss and the finding of the Boy, His ' first of miracles ' at Cana, His parting with her, the Passion, Calvary, the taking of His body from the Cross, the burial, Resurrection, Ascension, Pentecost, the daily Mass and Communion from the hands of St. John, were so many increasing moments of grace which deepened her floods of love.

II

Of course, that is precisely why her purity has been so celebrated, for purity means, as we have described already, a love of God, the positive dedication of one's self and one's friendship to Him, the making Him a third in all our human loves. Well, think of her love, and you see at once how He absorbed all her energies and powers. Mothers, in their extravagant language speak of ' worshipping ' their children; she certainly worshipped her Child, for He was also her God. Every inducement, human as well as divine, urged her to love Him increasingly, His beauty, His charm, the appealing winsomeness of His childhood, the quiet dignity of His growing manhood, His tender care of her, His strength and vision. Everything human and divine drew her to Him. This was the secret of her holiness, of all her virtues, not least of her purity. This last especially she had, because it was founded on an especial affection for Him. Her love of Him was so whole-hearted that no room was left for any other appeal to her desires; no evil attracted her, because she was already attracted wholly to Him.

III

Here, then, we shall find in Our Lady a great patroness against the temptations to impurity. She shows us the surer way, not of escape, but of prevention, for the firm remedy of these evils is a constant and devoted friendship with Christ. Without this we shall find ourselves entangled in endless miseries; with this everything falls into place. We must cling, therefore, to her support, to her intercession, to hold us nearer to her Son. In statues and paintings we find her represented as a Mother holding and delighting in her Child; so did she find her way to that high chastity that has made her an object of devotion to all those in trouble from the passions that stir the human heart. She soothes the perplexities of our nature by inspiring the primary dedication of ourselves to her Son. She lays her calm hand on us and stills our passion, quiets our excitement, by showing us how to centre ourselves upon Him. Our love for human friends will grow not less, but greater, when it is purged of selfishness, when the mere fleshly pleasure of it is ennobled by looking to a higher purpose, when through our friendship with Our Lord, itself deepened through our devotion to His Mother, we recognize the perfect beauty of her character, its inviolate purity, and we see in this no weakness but a towering strength.

FAITHFUL VIRGIN

I

Our lady is a help to us not merely in temptations against purity, but in other ways as well. After all, much as man may be troubled by sex problems or whatever we may care to call them, he has other difficulties to face. Impurity is not the only sin, nor is it the worst sin. We may easily get in the way of being obsessed by this one form of evil, and forget that it is merely one of many enemies with which we are at war. Indeed the Catholic Church has taught always, that though all sin is evil, spiritual sins are, on the whole, worse than carnal sins: that pride, for example, is more deadly and despair more destructive than sins of the flesh. Consequently we must look upon Our Lady not only as an example to us of chastity, but also of all the other virtues. Let us turn to her now under the invocation of the faithful Virgin.

II

Consider what is the noblest and most redeeming trait in human character. Probably not everyone would agree as to what they believed this to be. Some might take one and some another, perhaps gentleness, charity, a flaming love of justice, a stern sense of truth. Yet it does not seem unwarranted to say that, to judge from English literature, the most redeeming feature of a man or woman or child, is loyalty, consistency in devotion, fidelity to a trust. Success or failure naturally do not very much effect hero-worship. In fact, national heroes are often men who led a forlorn hope, who dared greatly and yet failed; but one thing alone is always said of them, that they were loyal to their cause. A renegade is always distrusted, a traitor is almost the worst name of insult, a turncoat is universally detested, even by the party he joins. We feel that loyalty is the fairest of human virtues, the most stirring, and, in an evil man, the most redeeming. Many, for example, of those historians who have most denounced Thomas Cromwell have gladly paid homage to his fidelity to his master, Wolsey, in the day of his disgrace. Again, the romantic glamour that surrounds with pathos the name of the royal house of Stuart, owes a great deal to the heroic loyalty of its supporters, and is no little tarnished by the corresponding lack of loyalty shown by the Stuarts to their friends. Those who by nature venerate that kingship are disconcerted by its desertion of Laud and Strafford in their moment of peril, and the many other instances in which it failed to repay with fidelity the fidelity shown to it.

III

The reason for this ready praise of fidelity in man is due to the half-conscious realization that it is foreign to his fallen nature. He is a creature of impulse and caprice, essentially subject to change, tempted incessantly to follow the way of fortune and fashion and self-interest. When, then, he sees constant loyalty, he is amazed and touched to reverence. He has come in contact with something that reminds him of the eternal steadfastness of God, who is without shadow of change. Our Lady is evidently a high example of this constancy; in the joy of His presence she loved Him, and when He left her to be about His Father's business, she learnt still to accept His will; even to Him on the Cross and dying, when the Shepherd was struck and the sheep scattered on the hill, she still remained faithful. Without murmur or complaint, her virginal heart clung to Him, faithful unto death. Through the Gospels He seems to deal her strange, unmerited blows that perplexed as well as hurt her; yet she accepted all, 'pondering over them in her heart', for of her, no less than of us, it was demanded that she should serve by way of faith only, blindly faithful, without knowing reason or purpose. Her sorrows, her loneliness when He had gone, her long wait for release, she patiently accepted because she was as full of faith as of grace, a 'faithful Virgin'.

HEALTH OF THE WEAK

I

IT was the great prerogative of the Mother of God to live with her Son for thirty years, to learn of Him the lessons of her life. She was to face suffering, the greater because of her love for Him whose sorrows would thereby become her own. All His action on her life in Bethlehem and Nazareth was to prepare her for this. The scene in the Temple shows us a glimpse of what must have been an unending schooling, laboured at day after day. The Mother has indeed left us no record of it, told us none of the intimate parables woven for her out of every-day occurrences; but such slight appearances as she makes in the Gospels are always accompanied by some saying of Our Lord in reference to the Divine Will. He was teaching her more and more to see life through His eyes, to accept it as He saw it, impressed with the inspiration and governance of the Father. Incessantly she was being taught by every fashion of lesson to see God's decree in all that befell her, to find Him everywhere in her life.

II

We can see this perhaps more clearly where it is least evident, on the Cross, in that mystic substitution of John for Himself: 'Behold thy Son'. Too often we are content to accept it merely from our point of view, the divine gift of us all in the person of the beloved disciple to her care. It is that of course; but it was directed actually to her and intended to open up for her the great lesson of her life in another form. Henceforward in every faithful follower she was to see her Son, each was to be to her another Christ. Is it straining a point to see a reference to this scene, in St. John's own principle that man is to be loved as the visible embodiment of God: 'For he that loveth not his brother whom he seeth, how can he love God whom he seeth not?' (1 John, iv, 20). He had gone, was no longer visible to her in the flesh, though every day she could yet be made one with Him in the Sacrament of Communion; she was, however, by faith, to find Him in all human creatures. He was handing them all over to her care, but precisely because she would see in them Himself. So closely was she made like Him, that she saw in the world what He saw, she by faith, though; He by sight. He loved all because He saw in them the mirrored image of Himself; she loved all because she saw in all His image mirrored: 'Mother, behold thy son—and henceforth the disciple took her to his own'. And henceforth too, she saw her Son in every human soul.

III

Now that is one reason why she has been so unswervingly the health of the weak. What can strengthen us, lift us above our narrow prejudices, take us out of the pitiful exclusiveness of our views of others, shake us free of the Pharisaism that would let the world that does not happen to be our world go its own way and face its own troubles alone, while we never stir a finger to help it ? We want a wide spirit, a kindly appreciation of all the world, a power to trace in human nature, however stunted, deformed, unspiritualized, the groundplan of that design on which it was originally built, the likeness of God. She is the Mother of us all, because in us all, even in the least of His brethren, she sees Himself. We can turn to her and ask her to implore with us of her Divine Son, that we may have her great vision of human souls. Not only in St. John, nor in the penitent Magdalen, did the Maiden Mother see Him reflected, but she found Him everywhere. Earlier, when He was told that she and His brethren stood on the edge of the crowd, He waved His hand over the crowd, its motley elements of sick and possessed and unclean, and declared that these were His mother and sister and brother; she learnt a higher lesson from Him, she found they were Himself.

LOVE OF LIFE

I

Our first duty, our first commandment, is the love of God. What does that imply? Not only must we love God, but we must love all God's gifts to us. 'Love me, love my dog', is a common proverb, full of useful meaning, for when we are fond of people our very fondness for them attaches itself to all that is theirs and makes us treasure even trivial things that are redolent of their personality or that carry memories of them. Consequently, once we realize that we have to love God, we realize also that we have to love all that is God's, especially all that comes to us from Him. We love His gifts, not because of what they are in themselves, but because they come to us from Him. With our friends the same thing is done. Their presents to us we treasure before we have undone the paper and string that hides them. It is not the gifts but their giver that makes them of such value to us. Consequently, when we look round and see that life (our life in its broad lines and details), comes to us from God as His greatest gift to us, then even before that life is clear to us, before we are aware of all it contains, before we have tasted or even guessed its bitterness, we must accept it absolutely and with love.

II

We have our life, then, from God; for that reason we must love it. We must not be in a hurry to judge it ill. Before we look at it we must suppose that it is good, for it comes to us from the hands of God. But why, if it is good, have we to suffer in life ? How can I honestly say that life is good, when I know that for many it is intolerably base and sad and sordid ? How can I complacently agree to these statements of the goodness of life when every day I am faced by the knowledge of the terrible lives of others ? Well, one thing at a time. Leave other people's lives alone for the moment: take your own. Theirs can be dealt with later. Here, then, before we look at our lives at all, we must start by saying that they are good because they come to us from

God. That is an act of faith, of course, but then, it is an act of faith which everybody is called upon to make who believes in God at all. As far as my life is concerned, then, I am called upon before I undo its paper and string, while, to vary the metaphor, I look wistfully out at it, ignorant (perhaps blissfully ignorant, of what it will bring), to say to myself that it is good because it comes from God's hands. But then it does not look like good always. It has all sorts of ugly corners and unpleasant moments and surprises that make me anything but happy. Yes, but all the same the truth remains that it does come from the hands of God, that is, from the hands of love.

III

That is where the Gospels can help us. You remember all those sayings of our Master when He spoke of sparrows falling, of death busy in the midst of life, of the tumults of existence, and assured us none the less that none of these things happened 'without your Father' (Matt. x, 29). The *Father*, mark you, as though He would have us remember that He was no less the Father even when He let these things befall. That is precisely where our faith comes in. We have to say to ourselves that He is the Father, that is, that there is tender love in Him, when His will lets things happen that bring pain. But how can I reconcile His Fatherhood with all this sadness? How can I? I have not to do that. That is His business, not mine. He has to reconcile them, not I. My part is very much simpler, mine is only to accept them without seeing at all how they harmonize. Of me the higher beatitude is asked, not seeing but believing. God is love, love is His only motive; once I believe in God at all, I must believe that His motives can only be good motives, for God is good.

GOD'S WILL

I

WE have already laid down the two principles (*a*) that God has a purpose for me; (*b*) that God wants me to carry out that purpose. There can be nothing far-fetched in either of these two. God is wise, then He acts for a purpose; God created my soul, then He has something for me to do. So far so good. Now since He has a purpose for me, it is clearly a purpose He wishes me to fulfil. But if He wishes me to do it, He will, therefore, make it clear to me. Moreover, since He knows my foolishness and blindness, He will —so to say—go out of His way to make it clear. Oh, He knows me through and through, knows how very easily I can mistake His meaning, and because He wants the thing done He will be telling me endlessly what He wants of me! But I find it difficult to know what His will is? Then

I can be sure that the fault does not lie with Him. He wants His will carried out—else it would not be His will; hence I can be sure that He is making it clear; and if it is not clear, the fault must be mine.

II

Have I, then, any way of finding out God's will? I am sure He must be illuminating me all day long, speaking to me in a thousand voices, yet I miss these hints and expressed desires. How can I learn where to look for them? He makes signs to me; how can I discover these signs? Well, perhaps it is not very easy to lay down laws about them, because God has a disconcerting way of treating each of us differently, so that drawing up a guide book is not very helpful when you are dealing with One who refuses to be reduced to little human tabulated statistical columns. Still, we can get a certain distance in the right direction by saying that these signs are of two sorts, within and without. First of all, take the signs within. God started us off in life with a certain bias of temperament. We have certain likes and dislikes, sympathies, antipathies, con-natural, born with us, beyond choice. *De gustibus non disputandum.* Why cannot you dispute about tastes? Chiefly because they are not a matter of reasoned argument, they are instinctive; you can correct them, modify them, sublimate them, but they remain. Now why have I this particular temperament? Evidently it was given me by God for some purpose. It will fit in perfectly with some design of His. Without it, I shall not be able to do the work He has designed for me. When faced then by alternatives, as to which is His will, I must first analyse my intuitions and examine my natural preferences. Presumably they are there for a purpose. But secondly, there are signs without, which we call circumstances. We are not perfectly free to follow our impulses and preferences. We are hampered by the world in which God has set us, the age, the stage of life. This also is of God, and may not be ignored. So life, then, is made up of two forces that fit in with each other, that check each other, modify, play into each other's hands and yet against each other. Impulse drives us, but is checked by circumstance; then when we are blocked, comes a fresh impulse, which again is blocked or deflected by circumstance; thus shepherded we are urged along the path which God would have us choose. He drives us by their inter-play. He drives well.

III

What is asked of us in this battle of impulse and circumstance? Three things chiefly: (*a*) a sensitiveness to God's call; (*b*) a cheerful humility that is not rooted in its own will; (*c*) a quiet and patient surrender not to self, but to the work and to God.

CIRCUMSTANCES

I

CIRCUMSTANCES are the scapegoat of the Failure. He always throws all the blame on them. He is no end of a fellow, but he has never had a chance. He bids you look at this and that other, what a success they are; but then, what wonderful chances they had. His whole philosophy lies there. Life is a medley of chances; if the opening happens to come, you can do something fine; if it does not, you never can. That is about as far as he can see into the brick wall of life. Then biographers and autobiographers play into his hand. You read a man's Life, saint or sinner, and you begin to believe in circumstances. You find the hero's birthplace and surroundings make him what he is one day to become; his down, country, or hills, or wild moors, gave him from the start the gifts he was one day to need; his ancestry explains so much of his success, explains it away even, so convincing is it all. His schooling has its place, of course; and then you are led right up to the breathless moment when his chance comes. He takes it—immense relief, you know he is a made man. Biographers do that sort of thing. It is their way. To their understanding, the hero, for all his heroism, is a mere puppet in the grip of forces beyond his control.

II

Now it is the easiest thing in the world, once you have got this idea into your head, to become a complete cynic. You have all the necessary ingredients to hand. You know perfectly well that whatever befell the lucky hero, it would help him on to pave his way to success, or turn up later and account for some curious accident that just saves him from ruin. In the end you rather wonder why he is a hero at all. He was merely a top that spun into fame because it bumped against the projecting side of wood, and got jockeyed into the hole which was marked with the big number. After all, you feel the biographer has made it altogether too easy. He has destroyed his hero's personality, left it out of account. Just so the failures we meet equally leave out the real cause of their troubles, namely not their circumstances, but themselves. We are so apt to blame every culprit but the right one, to blame circumstances instead of self.

III

Now the Christian lays down as his first principle that, since each has his own vocation, God-planned, the circumstances must always be favourable to that vocation. First, however, remember that the vocation is unending, goes on all life long, is bound not to the single choice of a profession, but all day and every day. God has a work for us at every moment, and consequently at every moment the circumstances are favourable to the carrying out of His will. God is just; He could not, therefore, fairly demand anything of us which the circumstances did not permit. But secondly, of course, we have to be patient if we are to carry out these purposes of our life. The man born blind had to wait all through boyhood to manhood before that moment came for which he was created and by which he will be to the end remembered. We must steadily push forward in life, every fresh advance will meet with a fresh difficulty, the line will never run quite straight ahead; but we must be on the look-out for God's opportunity, take it when it comes, never grumble that we have not had our chance, for we always have the chance to do at any given moment what God wants of us; finally, steeping ourselves in patience, waiting for Him without fret.

MY ROOM

I

AFTER all, a man needs to know how to rest, else he will never know properly how to work. St. Philip once laid it down as a great art that a man should learn how to waste time. We all do waste time, and indeed have to waste time; but it is only rarely that people have skill enough to waste time becomingly and to good purpose. A good athlete knows how to rest, else he will grow stale; a good scholar must know it, too; indeed, everyone must know it who is ever going to do much with his life. Enthusiasm is an essential quality of success, but enthusiasm implies other moments when its springs are relaxed, its power held limply, when a man waits. Now that is the greatest of difficulties very often; indeed, it would almost seem a lost art, to know how to wait. We are in such a desperate hurry that restfulness as a fine art has been ignored by a generation which lives with one eye on the clock, unable to attend to the matter in front of it because of some matter that will have to be dealt with in a few minutes. We act and at the same time plan what we shall do next, without pausing between our toils. Naturally we suffer from nerves.

II

Can we cure ourselves? We must cure ourselves or we shall perish. We shall become spent, used up, effete. It is sometimes supposed that nations fall behind in the race of life because they do nothing, because they are incurably lazy; but that laziness is the result of overwork, not of refusing to work. Civilizations break down only when they have reached too fierce a pace. That is where my faith can save me, for the faith properly understood, while it is a spur to action, is also a guide to thought: it gives me truths to brood over; it teaches me to contemplate. One of the troubles you will remember of your school-days was that you lived on top of everyone else. At first as a small boy, you rather liked that. You would not have known what to do if you had been left to yourself. But gradually, as you grew older and recovered your individuality, you felt the need of being by yourself, or at least getting away from the herd. You were becoming yourself and you needed your own personal surroundings. You were blessed at last in having your own room. It was a great day in your school life. It was a great day in your life altogether. A room to yourself is a place that can save your reason and your soul. After we have left boyhood there is hardly anything that we need more than that. It can be the centre of our life altogether.

III

Writers make a lot of fuss about the beauty of a garden, its charm, its quiet peace. Yet when all is said, nothing can compare with the beauty of a room. Our Lord knew how wonderful it can be when He bade us close the door and pray to our Father in secret (Matt. vi, 6). Prayer can be learnt in one's room and temptation there fought with victory. Around us are the weapons we have found always of help: our books, our familiar prayers, the marked passages that have on other occasions stood us in good stead; our hobbies, our collections, the photographs of our friends, the inspirations to goodness and cleanness and honesty and truth that we gather from the faces that look at us from the walls, our gallery of living and dead, our absent and vanished friends, and the other pictures that are full to us of real beauty: not pictures we have chosen because others praised them, but because we have found them and loved them for themselves. There is our crucifix. It has faced us in many moods. It will save us again. Our room quiets us after temptation and temper; can be a real temple of prayer to us, can show us God.

GAMES

I

At school, games are a passion; afterwards they are an interlude. Sometimes they are not even that. They are a necessary good, however, for most people, though it will not do to insist on them for everyone. Frequently in the press we read of distinguished people like Bernard Shaw giving public interviews and stating emphatically that they have never played any games at all, so that it is rather too much to say that games are essential to anybody or everybody. Undoubtedly we have a tendency as a nation to extol—perhaps exaggerate—their virtues and good effects, though as often as not we get beaten by other nations even in games that we have invented, or perfected, or made popular. Our public schools and universities certainly devote, not too much time, but too much interest to games, since public opinion in them seems to respect only the 'beefy' athlete. He has his purpose indeed, but his is not the only ideal of boyhood or boyish prowess, nor is it the highest, nor the most attractive, nor does it carry with it any special holiness. A school athlete can be as deceitful, as unclean, as tyrannical, as anybody else; when, however, he is better than his fellows, he can do more than anyone else to give a good tone to the school.

II

Games, then, are by no means a purely purifying process. They are that probably; they work off certain energies which might otherwise break out in less innocent ways; they are good for health, are an excuse for getting people out of doors, teach a fellow to control his temper, to restrain his tendency to lose heart when the game goes against him, encourage what we not unfairly call the sporting instinct. All that is true and admirable. But when you have left school? Often it is exceedingly difficult even for those who want to do so to find a chance to play games. For most people they are necessary, and they should be taken up as a corrective from the levelling and depressing work of one's profession. But they are an interlude. They are never the main business of life. Our work, whatever it is, should have our heart, our energies. That is the way we fulfill our primary human purpose; that alone is worth a man's whole while; that faithfully carried out, is the noblest patriotism of which we are capable. We benefit ourselves and our country best by steadfastly and keenly and devotedly working at our profession.

III

But watching games? People make a great deal of fuss about the vast crowds that watch matches and never play. But first of all, as things are, we can answer (*a*) that they have all played; (*b*) that quite a proportion of the younger ones do play from time to time; (*c*) that of the rest many never have a chance to play. They have neither the time nor the opportunity. Having said that we can further proceed to say that most people, especially working people, do a good deal of physical exercise during the day, and do not need the same energetic amusements that more sedentary folk require. The evil of merely watching games depends largely on how the other hours of the day are spent. If our work keeps us indoors we need out-of-door exercise to compensate us for this; but how that exercise is taken will depend on our preferences, and these in turn will probably depend on our skill. No one likes a game at which he is no good. No man has any real need, if he dislikes them, to take them up. It is much more fresh air that is of importance than the inducements we give ourselves for taking it. We go, after all, as we are led.

VANITY

I

We are all pretty vain, i.e., we take pleasure in the things we are good at. It is rather hard not to. Perhaps it would be impossible not to take pleasure when we succeed; certainly it would be foolish. If, then, it is almost impossible and certainly foolish not to be vain, why is it wrong? Vanity in this sense is not wrong, it is right; at least it is honest. What then is meant by the sin of vanity? Well, before answering that question, let us put the problem another way round. Supposing I take rather an interest in my personal appearance, is that wrong? No, there seems nothing wrong in that. Supposing I choose very carefully the clothes I think will suit me, with appropriate handkerchief and tie and socks. Is that wrong? It cannot be wrong, can it? For after all, what am I doing? I am trying to deal with God's gifts in God's way. I am God's handiwork, God's workmanship. Now I should, naturally, like my handiwork to be properly cared for, properly mounted, properly set off. That is only right and natural. But God presumably would wish the same. At least, one cannot think of any reason why He should not wish it. Consequently, it seems to be only fair to God to treat my appearance as best I can, and, for His sake, make the most of it.

II

But if that is so, what becomes of vanity as a sin set down among the list of sins in the examination of conscience list in almost every prayer book? Certainly vanity can be a sin; but the word vanity in English can be applied, often is applied, to all sorts of things that are not sins at all. Let us get quite clear on that point. There is no harm in taking care of my personal appearance, my hair and clothes and ties. Indeed, far from being harmless, it is the actual need due from me to God. Can there be vanity in it in the sinful meaning of the word? Yes, there can. How? When it is excessive. How? Excessive in time and in expense. If by taking so much care of myself I waste time which I ought to have devoted to other things, or if I spend on myself more money than I can afford, and have by me quantities of things that are really no use to me, this wastefulness of mine can become more or less grave, and may be therefore seriously sinful. Or again, my purpose may be evil. I may deck myself out deliberately in order to do harm to people's eyes and souls. This last is probably exceedingly rare; and in any case the sin committed is not a sin of vanity, but a deliberate occasion of impurity.

III

Lastly, vanity is wrong when it is withdrawing from God what is His due. To be vain does not mean merely that one takes pleasure in doing things well. That is natural, indeed, inevitable. Vanity as a sin consists in taking to oneself the credit which we know is due to God. To know that we succeed is not wrong; to be pleased because we succeed is not wrong; to be pleased because other people praise us for our success is not wrong; but to take the credit of the success and to ignore God's work in it would be foolish and criminal. Whatever we have done well, we have done through God's power; we are mere instruments, tools, in His service. It is His power that works through us, gives us the idea and the power to carry out the idea. Our Lady has given us the measure and rule of vanity. She did not scruple, humblest and most modest of maidens, to prophesy: 'Behold from henceforth all generations shall call me blessed'. It seemed unlikely, yet it has been true. However pleased she might have been by this, she knew, as we do, that her greatness came from Another, was the very gift of God: 'He that is mighty hath done great things to me and holy is His name' (Luke i, 48-49). With these words in your ear, look at your hair and your ties.

HYPOCRISY

I

THE worst thing in the world is to be a hypocrite, but it is also the most natural. It is very difficult not to be a hypocrite. In a way we are all hypocrites. It chiefly matters how much we are hypocrites. After all, we often say things we really do not mean; and we smile and are cheered when people pay us compliments which we know that they in turn do not mean. Life goes on in this way, and possibly could not well go on in any other. It is then, the simplest thing in the world to be a hypocrite. But perhaps that sort of hypocrisy does not matter; it is in such an unmoral way that it does not seem to affect men's lives at all. But it is clearly sinful when it busies itself about religion and drags in the sacred things of the Faith and God Himself, to cover up all manner of evil. For instance, when a man who is beset with many temptations and who gives way to them, and perhaps is known to his friends to do all this, keeps regularly to his weekly Confession and to Communion, is he not proved thereby to be a hypocrite? Let us try to face the problem, for to many people it is a real problem.

II

We will take a man who has troubles against purity or temperance, who gives way and who is known to give way, and yet who regularly attends Mass and the Sacraments. What can we say about him? Undoubtedly he may be a humbug. We can all agree on that. But is he necessarily a humbug? Surely not. Why not? Well, follow the argument. First he has these temptations and gives way to them. That is true. But suppose for a moment that he is fighting against them. Of course, to judge by his repeated failures, it does not look as though he were making efforts, but it were foolish to judge a man by the mere apparent lack of effort, the mere external failures of his life. It is true we know when he fails, but what we do not know is when he has succeeded. That is the worst of it: we cannot know. He can never tell us, for example, the times he has been tempted and struggled and come through. And if he does not tell us, we cannot learn. Let us suppose that he makes efforts, not a very wild surmise from what we know of our own experience and its record. Now what efforts can he make? Personal acts of will, of course, but what else? Surely he can go to the Sacraments?. The Sacraments undoubtedly were given us to help us, and without them we cannot get at life at all. So it comes to this, that here is this poor beggar who has to face his temptations and who finds them usually too much for him, yet who is still making efforts and approaching the Sacraments as part of the very efforts he is making. Now it is rather hard on him to dub him as a humbug just because he does not despair. He is a failure, but he refuses to consider that. At any rate he is not going to admit that he is also beyond hope.

III

No man, then, is a hypocrite, who, for all his sinfulness, yet strives and hopes for his final success. He approaches the Sacraments because he sees that his only chance lies that way. He endeavours to hoodwink no one, least of all himself or God. Only he refuses to give in; he refuses to bother his head over what people say about him; religion is too solemn a thing for him to give it up just when his need for it is sorest. No; to fail and yet to go to frequent Communion, that is not hypocrisy. Indeed, it is real manliness. Not to surrender, to refuse to give up making efforts, to refuse to be scared off Communion because people will have the impertinence to misjudge us or the narrow-mindedness to take scandal at us, why should anyone find this hard to believe or describe it as though it were dishonest? Sometimes the confessions of such a man are the best tonic a priest ever has. Such a long fight, so enduring a temper, makes for his edification. Such a confession or series of confessions makes a priest reverence the tried and faulty soul of his penitent very deeply indeed.

WORK

I

Somehow the word spoken by God at the beginning, when He drove Adam out from the paradise of delights, seems to have affected us in a sense contrary to God's apparent intention. When man was cursed and made to till the earth and wage war upon thorns and thistles, and learnt that only in the sweat of his brow would he find his bread, it was indeed implied that toil should accompany all work and drudgery be a necessary condition of it. But God cannot have meant by thus ordaining it that man should endeavour to escape toil in his work whenever he could possibly get out of it. Yet that seems to be the tendency of man as his culture proceeds. Everyone inclines to despise labour, to avoid it, to seek to persuade or cajole or pay others to do what he could easily have done, and indeed be the better for doing. That certainly was not the meaning of God's curse, for in another place in Scripture we find this other saying: 'And every man . . . hath power given to him . . . to rejoice in his labour. This is the gift of God' (Eccles., v, 18). It is important that we should take this second saying to heart, and use it to interpret the meaning of the first. Work is indeed a toil now, and a labour; it was not so in the beginning. Yet though now it be a labour, man can indeed rejoice in it, not only through faith, but even through the fascination of his work for him.

II

Besides, on the other hand, what a paralyzing effect machinery (man's invention, designed to save him trouble) has made on man's temper! He has, by a just use of his ingenuity, discovered increasingly a way to save himself much drudgery; he has been able more and more to hand over to docile and unresisting forces the hardest and most tiring part of his toil. He has invented labour-saving devices, ways of making life easier. All that is right and proper. It is the use of a talent for which otherwise God would have demanded an account. But with this has gone a tendency that has borne evil fruit, chiefly because the ideas that lay behind the directors of it have not been open to the light of the Faith. First, they have endeavoured through the use of a mechanical power to isolate themselves from the place of their labour; they have lived apart from it, and as a consequence, its inhuman powers have blotted from their memories the human instruments that attend it; this mechanical colouring, so to say, has affected the directors, so as unconsciously to degrade human workers into mere 'hands', not minds or souls. Nor have the workers remained untouched by this same infection; they have at times, it is true—particularly at the start—broken the machinery in mad riot; but now they have passed almost to reverence it, so that they see nothing degrading in serving a machine (nor is there anything degrading), though somehow they consider it degrading to serve a fellow-being. To enter the services of a propelled machine, is not despised; but to enter the service of a human family is considered beneath their dignity. Machines have out-distanced men.

III

Work, indeed, as a whole, has lost its sanctities, for not only must the workers' hours of toil be limited, rightly and properly, but the ideal is preached, that man's object should be to acquire, as quickly as possible, sufficient wealth to enable him no longer to toil at all. He is to rest on his labours; he is to grow rich quickly and never add another hour to his work. We have lived to see a disrelish for simple things, for personal things, for a man's working for the joy of working. Just as people go looking to be amused, instead of amusing themselves, so they wait for others to work for them instead of working for themselves. This means the loss of the dignity of labour. On the other hand, some are accused of living on the labours of others. But the question to be asked is not: ' Do I live on the labour of others?' (all must do that), but rather: ' What do I contribute to the work of the world ? ' This way alone can lie our salvation. To despise work, to escape it, to consider it beneath human effort, to exalt the man who has in his vigorous years ceased to labour, is to make our civilization turn down the slope to chaos, and bring us back full cycle to the old barbarism. It is the same doctrine which is being preached to capitalist and communist, to make the pirate to be a prince among us, to raise the standard of mere pillage and destruction above honest labour, to undo the work of civilization and Christendom. Faith, then, is needed that a man may *rejoice in his labour*, for ' this is the gift of God '.

THESE DEGENERATE DAYS

I

PERHAPS we are too quick to judge our age as evil unfairly, too fond of comparing it unfavourably with the ages ahead of it. Now, first, to look for evil is really to debase oneself. We can only keep our minds noble by searching always for the good. Moreover, secondly, there are certain thoughts that can help us to correct our wholesale unfavourable judgements and realize they are not justified by the material in front of us. First we can be sure that far less evil exists than seems to exist. It is the way of evil to make a great noise, whereas good is more silent. ' Frailty makes good copy, but the record of commonplace virtue has a limited circulation.' Evil flames into headlines and gets reported at full length, but the good is unheeded because, mark you, it is too common. When we hear at times of waves of crime, arising from the number of crimes of violence reported in our press, we should keep ourselves from panic, for after all, the unmurdered vastly outnumber the luckless murdered. Health is normal and therefore not talked of; ill-health is remembered painfully and makes its presence felt. Yet our moments of pain are outnumbered presumably by our moments of freedom from it. Nevertheless, we discuss far more our ill-health than our health. We should start therefore by remembering that evil always will fill a larger place in public notice than good does, precisely because good is the more common of the two; so that the very prominence given to evil is an eloquent testimony to the prevalence of goodness.

II

Again, often enough we confuse in our minds difference with defects. We criticize people freely only to realize on reconsideration that these people have done no more than differ from us on a mere point of view. The world is full of differences and was designed to be so by God; and its value depends upon the coexistence side by side of all these differences and their being merged in a larger whole, wherein each several part falls into place and completes its neighbour, and thereby fulfils the grand design. But surely as far as the Commandments are concerned, we must all come into line and not allow differences? True. All that is suggested here is that criticism does not always confine itself to differences of principle, but to differences in the application of principles. That is why advice is so rarely followed. It is usually only good for the man who gives it. It is an arrogation of infallibility to ourselves to dub others as evil who merely happen to differ from us where difference can be allowed.

III

Finally, we should remember that, after all, we are fallible and erring creatures, limited, able to attend only to a definite number of things at the same time. We have a large number of powers and capacities and a small amount of attention to be applied to them. Consequently, when we do apply ourselves with enthusiasm to one thing, we must correspondingly be limiting ourselves in other directions. 'You can't have everything' is a sufficient answer to those who are astonished at a lack of perfection in anyone else. Gifts imply a lack of other gifts. Perfection in one line implies imperfection in another. All the virtues may be rooted in charity or love of God, and may therefore be always coexistent in the soul; none the less, they are not equally expressed nor rooted to the same extent. Consequently we must be careful not to be irritated by evil or what looks like evil. It may only be a testimony to goodness in another direction. It is therefore possible to notice not the imperfection, but only the perfection which occasions it. To look for evil is debasing, to look for good is ennobling. Any fool recognizes folly: it takes a wise man to recognize wisdom. Nay, cannot we go further and say it makes a man wise to look for wisdom and know it when he sees it? And therefore, that it makes a man good to set him looking for goodness? After all, God does not presumably expect perfect things of us, but good things; and good things here are never perfect.

COURAGE

I

Courage is the most praised of the virtues and the least understood. Cowardice is the least attractive of vices and probably the most rare. More people own to cowardice than have it. What is courage ? It is certainly not the same as daring. By daring we mean almost foolhardiness, a boldness that knows nothing of fear, that disdains all risks. Daring faces all these things without fear. Now, courage is compatible with fear, and that marks the whole difference between them. Daring implies its absence, and courage is compatible with its presence. Daring men may be also courageous, but courageous men need not be daring, for daring is the result of temperament, whereas courage is the result of virtue. Daring is rarer than courage and not so meritorious, for one cannot help being daring, whereas one can help being courageous. Courage seems to be best defined as the act of a resolute will in the pursuance of duty and in the face or threat of known danger. It is an act of the will, and not a physical act, since it is an act of virtue; and is therefore compatible with physical shrinking. It must be exercised in the pursuance of duty, for the act of a dare-devil is distinguished against it by being performed out of sheer love of danger. To be too frightened to leap across a chasm is not a lack of courage, unless one is bound by one's duty to do it. Further, there must be known to be danger in the act done, else it might be done not out of courage, but out of mere ignorance, folly, or forgetfulness.

II

No one, therefore, is a coward except a man who, in the face or threat of known danger, shirks his duty. There are many people who in war, perhaps, will tell you they were cowards at heart. All they really mean is that they were afraid. Now a man may be afraid and yet despite his fear may do his duty. That is not cowardice but the highest courage. To be terrified of a horse or a dog or a madman would never be cowardly, unless we were to allow our feelings to prevail over our sense of duty. Courage, therefore, is compatible with fear and is most in evidence, perhaps, when fear is strongest. Consequently, we may know that at heart we are easily frightened; this is no fault of ours, it is usually the result of some old experience or of mere temperament.

III

What we have often to remember, therefore, when we find ourselves in difficulties, is that courage is a gift of God that urges us to continue our efforts despite failures and fears. If we have done our best we have this further assurance, that the result will not be as futile as we may think. We have done our duty in the face of discouragement, and even though what we aimed at has not been accomplished, we have not thereby failed. To have made the attempt is already to have achieved something; to continue to make attempts because we see that our duty lies that way, is an act of courage, and therefore, whether the results be disappointing or not the initial act remains in force. Success is only an accident due to the concurrence of other forces besides ourselves. We owe success, wherever it comes to us, to causes other than ourselves. Moreover, success without a check would weaken our character, and even our freedom. No people and no individual can remain free without a constant effort. It is this very effort that makes them worthy of freedom, and the freedom thus achieved, unless it requires repeated further defence, gravitates to weakness. Unused muscles grow flabby. Unused powers become atrophied. Opposition is the stern and kindly guardian of the soul. After all, opposition is even a tribute of flattery, for no unsuccessful work provokes opposition. So long as it is unsuccessful no one bothers to do more than to prophesy its end. In proportion to its success it offers a target to contradiction, ' gives hostages to fortune ', and therefore, only when it is disturbing or threatening to disturb other forces, human or diabolic, is it likely to meet contradiction. Temptation from the evil spirits is in consequence the best testimony to our success, and the more they are redoubled, the more full of hope should we grow; the fury of the fighting merely proclaiming that God's grace has been set around us. Our checks in life are a tribute to our power and God's mercy, and should nerve us to repeated efforts. Even when we have tried our best and failed, we can be sure that if we have not secured what we wanted, we have secured what God wanted. Our plans may have gone astray and yet our soul be no less great; and to continue our efforts, despite the past and in fear of the future, is courage indeed.

HONOUR

I

'What is honour? A word. What is that word honour? Air: a trim reckoning. Who hath it? He that died on Wednesday. Doth he feel it? No. Doth he hear it? No. Is it insensible then? Yea, to the dead. But will it not live with the living? No. Why? Detraction will not suffer it. Therefore I'll none of it. Honour is a mere scutcheon; and so ends the catechism.' So ends, indeed, the catechism of Falstaff. Not quite so brutally put, yet with much the same teaching, ends the catechism of a number of other people also. Honour is the most quoted and the least agreed-on word in the language. First of all, where does honour lie? The answer of most people is that it lies on the lips of others, not of the man himself. To most it is identified with a man's good name. His honour is said to suffer because people think or speak badly of him. Again, to speak of 'sharing honour' with a man is to use the word in a sense wholly different from that employed by Falstaff. We speak of 'national honour', or 'schoolboy honour', but we do not mean honour shown to the nation or to the schoolboy, but rather their moral conduct as measured by some external standard. A nation's honour is said to suffer when it disregards a pledge which it has given, or refuses from self-interest to defend an oppressed nationality, or itself oppresses a weaker neighbour or ill-governs its own citizens. We measure the nation's act against an ideal standard of honour and decide that it comes short of it. Schoolboy honour is another term which merely fixes a standard and decides whether individuals conform to its requirements or not.

II

But what strikes us, once we put the matter in this light (and it is from the same point of view that we talk of a man's honour) is that honourable conduct is settled by an ideal measure, over which people may be divided. A man's honour depends absolutely on his moral code and cannot be settled for him by fashion or popular opinion, unless he refuses to take the trouble to consider for himself what is honourable and what is not. Fashion, then, or popular opinion, are the alternatives to a fixed moral code, and fashion and public opinion have an extraordinary way of controlling people. Take, for example, the curious schoolboy honour with its fetishes and its taboos. Up to a point that honour is wonderful and inspiring; yet it has lapses that make it not only incomplete, but mischievous. It forbids tale-bearing, yet permits cribbing, considers snobbishness intolerable yet boasts of drink, would be aghast at the sight of brutality to women yet doesn't reckon as brutality the normal offences against womanhood, urges that men should fight only with others of their own size yet sees no cruelty in instructing a younger and more innocent boy in degradation or immorality under the specious name of friendship, and cloaks selfishness under the nasty practices of Greece. 'What is honour? Air: a trim reckoning.' So again, bills are left unpaid while money is wasted in other ways. Boys are generous in their 'debts of honour', yet may have little honour in their debts.

III

All the talk of a thing not 'being cricket', of a man not 'playing the game' is unconsciously an appeal to an artificial and amateur code which is as uneven as the code of the pagans and far more sacred than the code of the Popes. A Christian boy or man must aim higher than that. For him no code can be suitable that is not measured by the majestic height of Christ. This includes indeed the glory of ancient Rome, that venerable tradition of pride, of which a classic example is the story of the Senators on their curule chairs in the forum when the Goths entered to fire the city, sitting silent with the calm air of gods; but to pride like this, Our Lord now wedded a humility, a gentleness, a tenderness that the classics could not portray, a patient bearing of indignities, which has ennobled the squalid lives of the Christian martyrs and made ' the weak things confound the strong '. Humility, chastity, obedience, poverty, contempt of self, love of the brotherhood, the returning of good for evil, innocence, hunger and thirst after justice, truth and a high sense of duty, are some of the things that Christ included in His standard of honour, that are fragrant with His special perfume, vital and full of energy, that have moved men's minds and shaped their lives. ' He died on Wednesday, doth he feel it ? Doth he hear it ? Is it sensible, then ? Yea, to the dead.' But He that died on Friday felt it and heard it and was sensible to it. Yea, to that Dead and to His followers honour is a trust never betrayed.

HEAVEN

I

IT is a curious thing that Our Lord usually uses the word Heaven when He is talking of the earth. It figures in such an expression as the 'Kingdom of Heaven', and this means almost always the Church which He came to found here below. In the Pater Noster, indeed, He speaks of Heaven as the place where the Father dwells, but His chosen phrase when He is describing the joyous reward of the just is 'life everlasting' (Matt. xxv, 46). Now it is to be noted that in that passage last referred to, Our Lord speaks of Hell 'as everlasting punishment', but He does not speak of Heaven as 'everlasting reward'. Thus we are given a more detailed description of Heaven than of the other place; Hell is represented to us merely negatively whereas Heaven is set before us as 'everlasting life'.

II

We often speak of people that we meet or people of public character as having 'vitality' or life in an exceptional way; and we mean by that particularly that these people radiate round them an energy, or activity, almost a sunshine, immediately perceptible. Their coming into a room or on to a platform makes a difference to all present and creates an interest out of proportion to anything they have said or done. It is rather what they are than what they do that makes them exceptional. They can talk platitudes or do simple things, yet these are at once charged with new meaning and have a greater impressiveness merely because of the person from whom they come. But in saying this, we are describing the results of this vitality and are not touching its cause at all. What does it mean in itself? What would we say of these people themselves? Their vitality seems to be due to their greater consciousness of life, they are more awake than their fellows, they touch life at more points, are more responsive, more sensitive to everything around them, see what others miss. 'That fellow,' we say of some man, 'is only half awake,' and we mean by this, that about him things are happening which are lost on him because he is not on the look-out for them. On the contrary, those who abound with vitality have an eagerness that makes them go out to meet circumstances half way. Whatever happens near them they notice; their eyes are open; they are essentially awake. Hence it is too, that they awaken others. Briefly, then, vitality means intense consciousness of life. Man is charged with life in proportion to his awareness of life; he gives out what he has first stored up.

III

When, then, Our Lord speaks of Heaven as ' everlasting life ', we conclude that those in glory are alive because they are intensely conscious of life; they have vitality because they are awake. What are they awake to ? They ' live unto God ', they are awake to Him and He is very life: ' I am who am '. God is life, and heaven is defined as life everlasting because it means that a soul there is brought into touch with God in a particularly intimate way. But how can we be nearer to God than we are at present on earth ? God is everywhere and in everything; therefore He is within and close to us. Can He ever come closer ? No. He cannot. Heaven does not therefore mean that God is closer to us, only that we then see how close He is. He could not be nearer than now, but here we are blind, even the best must be blind to His nearness, since no man can see God and live. 'We walk by faith.' 'When did we see Thee naked and cold and hungry and thirsty?' is the puzzled question Our Lord puts on the lips of the good as well as of the evil; note that they ask when it was that they saw Him. Of course, that they never did. They believed Him to be present in His Brethren. They could not see that He was in the poor. Not sight, but faith, on earth; not faith, but sight in Heaven. That is the essential act of Heaven whence follow all its joys. Heaven, then, consists in a vision or an awareness of the life about one, and the life about one is God. It will be therefore a place intensely, eternally, alive. No question there of dullness or boredom, since souls see before them all truth and goodness and beauty, since all their powers find their fitting functions, since every desire is endlessly active and endlessly fulfilled. That vision, that awareness of life, that face-to-face consciousness of God, will be essentially the same for all; yet in the measure in which we have looked for God here, by some infinite rule of proportion, in that measure we shall find Him in Heaven. We shall know Him wholly and essentially, all of us who get there, yet not all equally comprehend Him. Our search and love for Him here will determine our finding and our love above. So Heaven, you see, is begun on earth, though none of us shall understand this till our earth days are finished and 'we know even as we are known'.

HELL

I

We have Our Blessed Lord's own words for it that Hell is 'everlasting punishment', and it is of more concern to know what Our Lord taught than to be able to make it fit in with our own preconceived notions of His mercy or His power. It is perfectly true that boundless mercy seems at first to imply that everything must be forgiveable, indeed in the end forgiven; but we have such difficulty in realizing to our imagination what is meant by eternity that no mere man here can understand what is meant by 'in the end'. Again, mercy is a virtue and not mere foolishness, for we see sometimes on earth, mistaken kindness which is more disastrous than many crimes. But after all, discussions about Hell, however interesting, are likely to be without result and are certainly of no consequence, since it is sufficient for us to know that Our Lord explicitly taught the existence of a state of eternal punishment. On that we must take our stand. If Christ revealed it, we must accept it, whether we can justify it or not. But did He teach it? How can we be certain that the phrase bears the meaning that we put on it? Of course, we cannot be certain unless we have an infallible guide to interpret Scripture for us, so that here as elsewhere we have either to leave the question undecided or find some authority to tell us exactly what Our Lord did mean.

II

Moreover, remember who it is that tells us of this terrible place: 'These shall go into everlasting punishment and the just into life everlasting' (Matt. xxv, 46). Now the speaker of these words is the kindest and the gentlest of the sons of men. Cannot we be sure that if anyone was sympathetic, not likely to view life narrowly, not harsh to sinners, it was He? If anyone thinks it incongruous for a God of mercy to punish sins for ever, and prides himself on so thinking, he would hardly claim to be more understanding than Christ. Yet it is precisely Christ who tells us of it. We have it not from the Apostles, but from Christ. But He is never unkind to sinners?

No, perhaps not; but He had a perfect hatred of sin. Kind to the sinner, He was full of anger to the sinner who thought he was a saint. He loathed sin with the force of His whole being, the vicarious contagion of it beat Him to the ground in the Garden, His purity of heart and love of His Father made it revolting to Him, though He would pardon it at once to the sinner who was contrite and realized the foulness of his sin. Sinners He loved, sin He hated. Does that help us to get a glimpse of the way in which He could accept and teach the doctrine of Hell? Suppose we could really understand the meanness and awfulness of sin, would that help us to understand the inevitableness of Hell? Can we hope to be able to reconcile our imagination to 'everlasting punishment' so long as we are unable properly and fully to grasp the evil of sin?

III

But do people really commit sin knowingly? Well, anyone who sins in indeliberate ignorance certainly will never be condemned to Hell for it. All that the Catholic Church has ever taught is this: those who die in hatred of God, having sinned gravely and knowing the gravity of their sin (unless their ignorance itself be gravely culpable), will be punished everlastingly. To say that none die like this, is beside the point, for who of us by human knowledge can answer whether they do or not? For us there are only two things to be said: first, we accept the doctrine for the one and only reason, that we are taught it by Christ, secondly, we should not forget this teaching of Our Lord, for it is never safe, honest, or manly to ignore the truth. We need not often call in the use of fear to help us, since the love of God must chiefly lead us; but love itself needs the instinct of fear and reverence, else it becomes mere emotion or mere passion, misses the austerity of strength. 'The Lord of terrible aspect' is the name given to love by one of the world's great lovers and he speaks here of divine as well as human love. And the conclusion to all this? What can one say better than the very words of Christ?. 'Strive then to enter by the narrow gate.' Hell means essentially the loss of God. Take care to find Him for ever hereafter.

PURGATORY

I

WHAT a very little we know about our future life! As Catholics we are taught less about it than many other religious bodies; we have no minute details given us such as spiritualists so dogmatically teach. We do not accept any of their elaborate descriptions, since they are largely and manifestly coloured by the imagination of the particular teacher and no less by the limits of his imagination. One, who is a clergyman, has depicted the next life for us in terms of a country vicarage: as narrow and stuffy an after life as he only would dream of who had never left the parsonage, surrounded by its own garden, with its clean bathroom, its spotless linen, and its work-parties. Another, who is a doctor, sets out just the hereafter which a doctor would guess at, seen through his interests, his sympathetic attempts to get rid of pain. A third, a physicist, gives us a very material idea of the abode of the dead, with scientific substitutes for drink and smoking-materials, and a strange hesitating desire for Ford cars. All rather pathetic when you think of it; interesting for the psychologist who compares the prophet with his profession and finds so close a tie between them and who cannot but regret that this should impose on eager people who pry morbidly into shrines that God has hidden from our eyes. All who speak must use human language and even Catholic saints and poets are not immune from this law. The revelations of the one, the dreams of the other, are interesting and suggestive, but not very helpful. They lead us no nearer to the truth than we were before.

II

The Catholic Church teaches very simply, both of Heaven and Hell, that the joys of the one and the pains of the other are beyond description, since the first means the vision of an infinite God, and the second the loss of that vision, both in terms not of time but of eternity. We cannot imagine either one or the other; we had far better leave them both alone and make no efforts to guess their implications beyond the facts of the possession of God as Heaven and the loss of God as Hell. Though our understanding of Purgatory is not hedged about with the same difficulties, since it is neither eternal nor deals with the vision or loss of an infinite God, it is nevertheless, almost as mysterious to us as the others are, because God has chosen to reveal very little about it. We have hardly any conception of what it means, except in general outline. We know, of course, as the name which we give it implies, that it is a place or state of cleansing, through which pass only those souls who have been judged worthy of Heaven, but yet are not worthy of immediate entrance into it. God is so absolutely perfect, the vision of God is so overwhelming, sin even in its least form is so terribly disfiguring, the divine justice must be so devouring, that to go straight into Heaven must be reserved for the soul when wholly cleansed both from the guilt of sin and from its due expiation; only so can it attain the blessed vision of God. Purgatory is the name we give, then, to that process of purgation whereby guilt and expiation are consummated together and the soul made fit to see God face to face. Cleansing implies some pain, submission to some process of destruction; expiation also implies suffering, the payment of a debt, the giving back of what has been withheld.

III

Yet Purgatory is a place of joy and not of sorrow. The souls in the process of their cleansing are not in perfect peace; they yearn for and desire the vision that lies ahead of them, and therefore remain serenely in that process gladly accepting what they know to be the only means of reaching their goal. The suffering is a joyous suffering, dictated by justice, accepted by love, and known to be required by God's glory. Yet God has softened even this for us by a wonderful disposition of His mercy. He has made it possible for us on earth to shoulder something of the pains they suffer who are in Purgatory; He has extended the claims and desires of friendship till they affect even the life hereafter. To our friends on earth we are always eager to offer our services if in any way it is possible for us to relieve them of any trouble, putting ourselves out gladly in order to put them at their ease. God has mercifully allowed us, by a sheer act of His good will, to bear the burdens of the dead. We can pray for them, that their process of purgation may be swifter; we can, as members of one mystic body of Christ, pass on to them the Indulgences we gain; above all, we can offer for them patiently and in courageous silence our aches and pains, our disappointments, the drudgery of our work and profession, the sting of the weather, the normal and abnormal sufferings of human life. The thought of our dead is not only pitiful, but bracing. In memory of them we are touched to tears, yet our tears are wiped from our eyes, and our moaning is hushed to silence, for the silence will help them more than moaning. We can offer for them all life's ills.

DEATH

I

IT is the repeated cry of Don Quixote whenever faced with a perplexing difficulty, that there is a remedy for everything but death. All else can be solved: only death is beyond our cure. It is this that strikes everyone, the finality of death, its unfathomable mysteries, its inevitableness. All else can be warded off with skill and persistence and high courage. But against death nothing can prevail. For that reason men do not discuss it. It hardly is a safe discussion. You can hardly discuss the problem of sunrise or sunset, hardly dispute about the fall of the leaves. Death is much too definite to be argued about; when you have mentioned its name you have said all there is to say about it. No, not quite all; for though death is quite clear, everything that precedes it and follows it is obscure. 'It is appointed unto man once to die.' That is about all one can be sure of, the rest is hidden from us, time, method and result.

II

We very naturally dread death and dislike the idea of its approach. Is it wrong? Should not a Christian 'desire to be dissolved and to be one, with Christ'? Is not death, to one who believes in God and a future life, a blessed release? Should it not be longed for? Yet we do not find in our hearts any such longing. Is it wrong? Even if it be wrong, perhaps, do we see how it can be helped? Certainly it would not be honest to say that we want to die when we do not. Before answering this question let us remember that in some moods other people have an exactly opposite trouble. A priest in the confessional will sometimes hear this self-accusation from a penitent: 'I have wished I were dead'. Evidently under the stress of misery of some kind, they have had a hatred of life and a desire to end all by leaving it. In such a mood is it that the poor suicide can see death only as the door of hope into a new world. At least he probably does not think of the new life; he is only anxious to be rid of the old. The canon against self-murder is God's refusal to

THE SPACE OF LIFE BETWEEN

accept anyone's haste to be out of life: so that cowardly desire for life's ending has to be balanced against the idea that a Christian ought to desire death. We can say, that in some sense a Christian should desire to die, and in some sense it is wrong for him to desire it. This juxtaposition of opposite ideas about the desire for death will help us to see our way through the difficulty, viz., on the one hand we guess that a Christian ought to want to die, yet we cannot honestly say we have any such idea; on the other, people who passionately desire death, feel convinced they ought not to desire it and confess it as a fault. We feel we ought to desire it, we feel we ought not to: who shall unriddle this?

III

The simplest way to unriddle most things is to leave them alone. Begin at the other end. Start by remembering that your life is a gift to you from God. That is certain. Well, because it is God's gift to you, you ought to think highly of it and value it. It is to be used, like all God's other gifts, in His love and service. It is a talent, and therefore, if not used to the full, will be requited against us at the judgement-day. Now does that help you? It shows you at once that you ought not, from God's point of view, to desire to die, to desire to end God's gift: ' the night cometh wherein no man can work '. So we ought to be in no hurry for the daylight to end. We ought to labour at the work He has given us to do, and we need life to be able to labour at it. If then, we have this gift of God, is it surprising that we do not want to give it up? Can it be wrong of us if we have to say honestly that we do not want to give it up? It seems indeed that it is the only thing we can say, namely, that we want to keep this gift of God, our life, and enjoy it, and use it to the full. But the Saints? That does not seem to be their view. Wait a minute. Supposing we take the Saints; cannot we be sure of this, that all they wanted was to do God's will? We can be sure of that. When, then, they spoke of their ' desire to be with Christ ', they meant that they loved God and wished to see Him face to face, that they found by contrast that earthly life did not content them, was inadequate to their desires, inspired them with nobler hopes of a finer world. All they wanted was to do God's will; but they did not find that this life satisfied them. The same is true of all of us. We often feel that we would like to be spared to see this or that finished, we pray that this or that person may be allowed to live for the sake of the work he is doing, or the family or the friends who depend on him; we ask to be allowed to live because life is sweet to us, is full of interest, beauty, love. Why not, indeed ? To wish to live is politeness to God for what He has given us, gratitude, an appreciation of His kindness. Yet all the while we are willing to accept His divine will, Who knows better our needs and chances. We enjoy what He gives, yet are desirous only of what His will determines. At times we long for the peace and joy that will follow on life's ending; at times we are thrilled by its present pleasures. Neither is wrong, so long as beneath our desire comes acceptance of His will: ' My soul is sorrowful even unto death. . . . Father, if it be possible, let this Chalice pass . . . nevertheless not My will but Thine be done '. A dread of death is compatible with perfect love. At the prime of life His body cried out against its ending, but the greatness of the soul triumphed in its acceptance of God's will.

HAPPINESS

I

We dread death for the same reason that children dislike going to bed; we are happy, and therefore want to retain our happiness. To go to bed seemed such a waste of time when other people were remaining up; to die seems hard on us when other people remain alive. We disliked going to our solitary bedroom when we could hear all the laughter below us and the clatter of dishes downstairs. It seemed unfair. So again we feel we have the right to happiness and yet do not always possess happiness. What do we mean by this happiness that we all pursue? It lies in so many different things. We are always chasing it. We sometimes find it. Even then we are troubled for fear it should not last. We must seek it. We cannot help ourselves. The pleasure seeker, of course, is after it; but no less in pursuit of it comes the man with a sense of duty. He gives up pleasure, he tells you, and devotes himself to live laborious days. But he knows that he ought to do this. It is not, of course, that he loves pleasure less, but that he loves duty more. The moral contentment and ease of conscience is not the prime motive of his action but the one sufficiently present to him to make his heroic resolve constitute his happiness. The emaciated Saint who seeks penance and solitude does indeed enjoy these things quite truly. To take penance sourly is no way of the Saints. Even the Saviour of the world did not face His Passion grimly. The temptation to reluctance He fought and quelled in the Garden, and rose in the strength of His triumph, a man, erect and free. We must think of Him going radiantly through it, joy shining in His eyes, love supporting His pains (' greater love than this hath no man '), and despite the pains that love caused Him, by some subtle paradox, these in no wise diminished the pleasure that love brought. It is true to say ' greater joy than this no man hath, that that He should be able to lay down His life for His friends '.

II

Are we then only selfish ? Are even the best

of us like the worst, pleasure seekers? Does the only difference between them lie in the difference of the pleasures they seek? If it be so, then we are a very poor race, without ideals or generosity, wholly self-seeking. One has only to say this to know that it cannot be true. We may be tripped up by the argument and unable to reply to it, but our instincts assure us that this cannot be and our instincts are true. We know that some people are unselfish and some selfish, and no sophistry of argument will ever convince us that both are the same. Yet we cannot deny that virtue does please the Saint, and vice the sinner, nor can we deny that both are seeking what pleases them. But really what does it all lead to? Only this, that both are seeking happiness. Well, of course, that is evident. Everyone must seek happiness. No one can help that, because we were made for happiness, and are restless till we find it. But there are gruff people who never seem to be capable of happiness, who always grumble, who never even suppose happiness to be possible. Oh yes, they really look for it, and indeed find it in grumbling: like the old jest of the people who ' enjoy bad health '. Everyone seeks for happiness, and must seek for it.

III

Really, everyone was made for God; without Him they are restless. They look for whatever will suit them, looking for something always, since whatever be given is always insufficient for one who was made for infinite goodness and truth and beauty. Man, we suppose, was made for God. God is his purpose. Granted that, it must follow that man will first never be content with less, and secondly, will always be looking for more. Hence all look for happiness. Does this mean all are selfish ? It depends on what exactly selfishness is taken to imply. If by selfishness we only mean that each looks for his completion and development, then we are selfish and ought to be. If we mean that we seek our completion regardless of other people and regardless of its cost to them, then we are selfish in an evil sense, and are wrong. We must seek our development and completion, seek to be wholly ourselves, seek to fulfil as nearly as we can our capabilities, and we must do this, partly driven from within by impulse, and partly deliberately dedicating ourselves to the Divine purpose which gave us these very capabilities to enable us to carry out our corresponding work. We love ourselves for God's sake. We shall no less remember our brother's interest and self-development, and moved by the example of

Christ, shall try to fulfil our purpose at no one's expense. Human as we are, we shall sometimes have to use our reason and our conscience, to decide whether to insist on our self-development or efface it for the sake of God. Thus Christ our God came back from the Temple to be subject to His Mother in Nazareth, and later left Nazareth sacrificing His Mother to His work.

ANGELS

I

One of the most difficult things to understand is how the angels came to fall into sin. They had perfectly equipped intelligences and must have known the evil of sin, and foreseen the disadvantages and results of rebelling against God. What chance had they against Him? Even pride 'by which fell the angels' ought not to have blinded them to the immeasurable distance between themselves and Him. But evidently it did blind them. There was war in Heaven. Lucifer the Light-bearer, one of the leaders of the host, headed and inspired the revolting angels against God. There could only be one issue to such a combat. The evil spirits were cast out of Heaven and the loyal angels were rewarded, as are all those whom God rewards, beyond their deserts. Does this mean that the expelled angels had once possessed and were now being driven from the enjoyment of the vision of God ? No, certainly not. No one could sin who has ever seen Him face to face. Before the battle therefore, the angels were in some state of trial; the battle was their trial; no other chance seems to have been vouchsafed them: the faithful were rewarded with the eternal vision of God, the faithless were punished for ever. That was the sole climax of their lives.

II

The aim of the evil angels has since been to tempt men away from their due service to God because of the hatred they have ever since borne Him. They use every subterfuge that will help them to achieve their object, masquerading under any form that best assists them according to the popular fashion of the day, whether it be art or literature or religion, or spiritism or science or social theory or wealth. But the loyal spirits, who preferred God's service have been no less active and more powerful. Some ' post o'er land and ocean without rest '. They are God's messengers, which is exactly what the word angel means. They do His bidding. And what does He bid ? He bids the continuance and development of the world, and to the furtherance of this uses the angelic powers; behind the natural movements of stars and winds, the precipitation of crystals, evolution and growth of trees and moss and flowers, setting in order the feathers of the wing, sustaining flight and motion, giving eagerness and vitality to the beasts of the field and the forest, numbering the hairs of man and set in charge over him, holding commerce with other worlds than ours, imparting to everything the power it needs, they severally perform God's work according to His purpose. What English law called 'the acts of God', are done by the ministration of angels; and even the acts of man, deliberate or of hazard, are carried through by the interposition of angelic force, directed at times by the free-will of man: for man fatally may use God's power to the undoing of God's plan. So His omnipotence had ordained.

III

Not only, then, have we guardian spirits, to attend us, but so has every other thing as well. And these guardians not only inspire their wards to follow the plan of Providence, freely if rational, by compulsion if not rational, but protect their wards against the aggression of others. Our Lord tells us that the angels of children see always the face of the Father. They are therefore directly able to intercede for the living. More than that; Our Lord says it were better for those who scandalize these little ones to have been hurled, weighted with heavy stones, into the sea, than to have done them harm, implying that the intervention of the angels will produce more terrible chastisements. We have wide and ample vision of a world alive and thronged with divine messengers. We see each flower and star, each leaf and hair, daintily and strongly held by the sentries of God. We find the universe, with its worlds beyond our world, with such inhabitants as they may have, bound together with an endless stream of presences, incorporeal, blessed, passing onwards the divine message, till it reaches the soul for which it is designed, and then carrying back the offering of the creature, its dutiful service, to the God who rightfully claims it. 'All the orders of nature, all the revolution of history, cycle upon cycle, in ever new types' are made active through the ministrations of these angels. Fra Angelico sees mystically the light upon their many-coloured wings as he walks in the garden of the Medici, the birds echo the songs of these blessed ones, the flowers reflect the broken gleams of their glory, the sun streams with the sparkling of their crowns, the waters break into diamonds, scatter and meet again, rainbowing and then melting back into pure white light that is no less than the splendour of their streaming robes, radiant, light-bearing veils that softened to weak human sight the dazzling splendour of God. Do not think of this merely as though it were poetic nonsense, the day dreams of a child. Expressed through the only medium that art knows, it transcended that medium and became a true vision. Truly, through the artist's eyes we see the true vision of the world.

SAINTS

I

GOD, we say, is wonderful in His Saints, and in so saying, though we may mistranslate Scripture, we yet state a truth, for God is made full of wonder to us when we see His Saints. A Saint is a sinner who is conscious of sins, who is sorry for sins and who seeks God. Is there anything very wonderful about that? Indeed there is. To be conscious of one's sins is a grace of God. It is He alone who can show up to us the dark places of the soul, and by this means the contrast between ourselves and Him dwarfs our goodness to insignificance and deepens the shadows of our sin. That is God's way of dealing with those whom He loves and whom He intends should love Him. In the lives of the Saints, whether of those who have strayed from God or of those who have never left Him, you will find how, with growing clearness, they saw their failures and the evils in their lives. But the Saints in so doing were not led to despair. They were not only conscious of their sins, but sorry for them. Now this is the positive side of sanctity. It faces facts without weakening under the self-revelation they produce. To be conscious of one's sin is indeed a grace of God, but others besides Saints have received it. Modern literature is full of that consciousness. Blanco Posnet is aware of his sin, and the author of *De Profundis* and even Barbellion found it stabbing them with a sudden pain. But sorrow for sin is none the less a gift of God, because it implies unselfish sorrow, the sorrow begotten of love and burgeoning into love. To regret the past with shame, need not be sorrow, unless with it runs a wistfulness of soul that turns away from self and is urged forward to further love. Hence, beyond consciousness of sin and sorrow for it, saintship implies a seeking for God. But does the mere seeking for God make a Saint, even though it follows on sorrow for sin ? Yes, it does, for the Saints are the lovers of God. All who are His lovers are His Saints. A mere seeking after God will do this ? A seeking if it be real and persistent, is a finding, for no one goes to look for God who has not already found Him; whoever looks for God must first have missed

Him, and to have missed God is already to have had some knowledge of what He means to the soul, and to have had some knowledge of what He is, is already to have dimly found Him.

II

God wonderful in His Saints? Of course He is wonderful, because His greatness is made manifest to us through them. They are but broken lights of Him, and He is more than they. Their goodness is a mere fragment of His goodness, a participation in it, a reflection of it. Since, then, God Himself in His immensity is infinite, our only chance of finding any contact with Him is to see Him in what He does. The sun is too dazzling to be looked at in its full splendour, but the divided colours of the spectrum gives us an idea, inadequate indeed, but suggestive of the glory of the whole. In some such fashion, the Saints, distinct and individual, representing in diverse and varied forms His perfect Being, inadequately indeed, yet suggestively reveal Him to us.

III

Of course, the bigger the City is to which men journey, the more roads must there be that lead to it. The little village, that straggles along a single high road, has but the ends of its one street to guide men to it. But the great cities of the world have numberless approaches. So it is with God. Immense beyond human categories, He must be a centre of roads as infinite in number as Himself; a city set high on a hill, the beacon of the wise, sought by souls whom no man can number, must necessarily be approached by each in his or her own way. We come to Him by the way He chooses for us, and whosoever cometh by whatsoever road was chosen for him, God will not cast out. God is really made wonderful to us in His Saints; their variety of goodness enables us to grasp better what God is like. Hope, too, is to be found in them, hope for others and for ourselves. We can hope when we see how each of them has climbed to God along a separate path. Of all ages, trades and nations, of all kinds of culture, learned and unlearned, of all degrees of moral excellence, we find only one common likeness in them: that they all (save one only) have been sinners and conscious of their sin and sorry for it, and have been seekers after God.

IDEALS

I

LIFE is all very well, but it never lives up to its own suggestions. Every man has had his ambition, or at least, hopes. He has looked forward to some future beyond his actual work of the day. He thinks his life will lead somewhere near what he has aimed at. Man has the faculty of discerning a wider horizon than the present, he looks before and after; he plans and labours and compares. That is because of his faculty of reason, and his powers of memory and imagination. Before he ever works, he has something set in his mind, a picture of what he is to produce. The architect with his plan, the artist with his cartoon and studies, the sculptor with his clay-model, forecast their work; so it is with a man beginning to face life. He sees a limitless future before him, and out of it chooses that life which shall be his. Nor does he aim only at something that he must do, but at something that he must be. He has surely somewhere in history or in fiction found a hero, his ideal character. To be impressed by a character is to have found an ideal; not of course, that we always wish to be like those whom we admire, but we must wish when we admire anyone that some gift of theirs were ours.

II

We have, then, our ideals for ourselves, what we would wish to be; now we shall be told that this is a foolish thing, because we shall find as we grow older that idealism is impossible, that nature cannot be changed, that experience will drive in on us the necessity of leaving well alone, not expecting too much out of life, nor aiming too high: being sensible people, taking the world as we find it. It is quite possible that experience will have this effect upon us; certainly no one will deny that experience does have this effect upon a number of people. We can see them start out (or perhaps they will tell us that they did start out), lit up with this idealism, but gradually finding the difficulties in the way of its achievement too stubborn to be removed, and finally accepting contentedly lower terms and lesser results. It is true, then, that experience can destroy young idealism; let us admit, however, that it need not. Let us admit even more than this, that the idealists alone have moved and benefited the world. Certainly experience can affect us. But what is experience after all? It is only what a man finds up against him in life, of good and evil. Experience, therefore, can be a very narrowing thing. We know some of the answers of experience: 'But we have always done this', or: 'We have never done that before'. This is indeed an argument, but not a final argument; it should not be used to block inevitably all further attempts. Progress of development is nearly always the triumph of 'persistive constancy' over experience.

III

Our Lord, who transformed the world, is the world's greatest idealist. He advocated what experience pooh-poohed. He talked about losing life to find it, becoming poor in order to lay up riches, becoming a child in order to understand the wisdom of God. Nor did He merely talk like that, He did those things. And to become like a child, what is it, but to reject experience? A child has none. But idealists lead lonely lives?

THE SPACE OF LIFE BETWEEN

They have to depend on themselves and be prepared to find themselves hated by the crowd: 'Lady,' said King Arthur to Queen Guinevere, 'it will behove me to go all armed and without knights'. 'Sir,' saith she, 'You may well take with you one knight and one squire.' 'Lady,' saith the King, 'That durst not I, for the place is perilous, and the more folk one should take hither, the fewer adventures there should he find.' One greater than all has confessed publicly to all mankind: 'Behold the hour cometh and it is now come that you shall be scattered every man to his own and shall leave Me alone; and yet I am not alone because the Father is with Me' (John xvi, 32). That is the loneliness of idealism and that also the remedy against it. We shall be left to ourselves? Perhaps; but at least the Father is with us, who is greater than all. Alone with Him we have adventures; 'the more folk one should take, the fewer adventures he should find'

LOYALTY

I

ONE thing to remember is that loyalty is a virtue. Sometimes people talk as though it were mere sentiment, of no concern to good practical men. Probably we use the word in many different senses and in none very accurately. Often enough by loyalty we mean very little else than jingo-patriotism. Often, again, we are begged to show our loyalty and gratitude (for the words are sometimes confused) by siding for this or voting for that, or at least not to proclaim our divergence from this or that, because of old loyalties. For their sake we should be silent. Perhaps this is urged properly in circumstances that justify such an appeal to us; but it is not always a valid argument. It is an attempt to stifle reason at the bidding of emotion, or it is an appeal away from experience to an ancient prejudice or the intrusion of a personal element into the impersonal domain of justice. Loyalty, then, is a virtue, which like others of its kind, can be put to false uses. Loyalty is a virtue; but it can be the cloak to prejudice and partiality.

II

Yet we feel that certain things or causes have a claim on us, in memory of past benefits or old friendships or the glory of a great history. Can a man, under these circumstances, be impartial? Should a man be impartial? Is it justice to treat an old friend quite as one would treat an acquaintance or a stranger? Is it wrong to be prejudiced in favour of one's own nation? Can favours accepted from the hands of another leave us quite as we were before? Does not loyalty compel us sometimes to refuse to listen to accusations? Does not it pledge us to defend our friends even when we know they have been at fault? Must one not out of love of country, rally to that country's aid, even in difficulties which her own misconduct has produced? The question is a practical one. What answers can be given? Well, first of all we must lay down as a principle that one of the ways in which we can share in the guilt of another's sin is by defending the ill done.

That is certainly the Catholic doctrine to be found in the catechism, so that whatever loyalty means, it cannot mean that we are to defend the ill done in the name of friendship, gratitude or patriotism. What, then, should loyalty mean to us? If I am not to defend the ill-doing of my friend, and can only defend his good actions, what is the good of loyalty, for after all, I must defend the good actions of everyone, even of enemies? It may be difficult to put into words exactly what is meant, but loyalty must imply certain obligations on me. I must be loyal to my country, i.e., I cannot treat her merely on business lines. It does not mean 'my country right or wrong', namely, that I must side with my country in her quarrels even if she is not in the right; it does mean, I must side with my country in her just quarrels, whether she has been just to me or no. So did the Catholics rally to the forces of Elizabeth against the Armada of Spain, in virtue of some mystical claim on them irrespective of what had been done to them.

III

Christ Our Lord, the Redeemer of the world, held fast by these loyalties. He wept over Jerusalem; we do not know that He wept over Rome. His teaching has served to deepen the sense of loyalty. He was Himself most loyal to whomsoever He had called by the name of friend: to Judas, to Peter, to the Magdalen. To the Jewish priesthood He was loyal, to the Roman rulers of His people, to the great story of Israel. Yet He was no respecter of persons, and spoke the truth to all, to those who trusted to their Jewish descent for salvation, to those who sat in the seats of Moses, to the traffickers in the Temple, to the priests, to Rome. Loyalty was a marked feature of His Life. Let us describe loyalty, then, not so much as a sentiment as an inspiration; not a reasonable philosophy, but a faith. It means that gratitude, friendship, relationship, patriotism, have sacred claims on us that nothing can ever set aside, though none of these claims can ever take us from our obligation to support truth and justice, on whichever side they are. Putting these aside then (that is, never acting in their prejudice), we must be loyal in our service, loyal in thought, in word, in act; offering spontaneously and not waiting to be asked, giving ungrudgingly, silently without reserve.

MIRACLES

I

It is a great blessedness for us that we live in a scientific age. By means of the microscope, we have been able to isolate and observe the existence and development of many creatures never before known; we have been able to learn more even of things whose existence we already knew. But it is of less consequence to watch closely the habits of creatures new to us, or to discover the constituent elements of inorganic matter, than to register the laws that govern these habits and elements. By careful and patient observation the great scientific minds have discovered and disclosed some of the laws governing the world, the law of gravity for example, the laws of motion, the chemical actions and reactions. These are rightly described as laws, since they would seem to be unalterable. Man cannot violate them, he cannot prevent the impulse that drives each thing of its own nature to fulfil its own destiny; but though he cannot violate a law of nature, he can, by understanding it, modify it or neutralize it, in virtue of another law; indeed, civilization is little more than a record of this. Man cannot oppose the wind with his sailing ships, but he knows how, by tacking, to avoid its force. There is a law that whatever is heavier than water must sink, yet man builds iron ships, heavier than the water they displace, and with them navigates the ocean. The law of gravity pulls everything to earth, yet by means of a propeller man drives his aeroplane upwards, towards the clouds and beyond them. By his mind, he can forcibly hold down and get the better of pain, bow it to his will. The world is not lawless, nor is man a rebel in the midst of the world; he can only use Nature by understanding her, obeying her inexorable laws, modifying some tendency that would do him harm, by balancing its action by some other law.

II

Now if man can, by means of one law of Nature, counteract another, is it fantastic to suppose that God can do the like? After all, it is God's own world. He made it and it is His. He rules and governs it with His divine Providence, so that no sparrow falls except by His will, so that the lilies of the field, without their labour, are arrayed beyond the glories of Solomon. In this world, then, of God's making, God Himself presides. He respects the laws of His own creation, He does not destroy but fulfil. He works, we claim, miracles when the need is, though they cannot be miracles to Him, since ' He giveth to all life and health and all things ' (Acts xvii, 25). By the word miracle we mean something done by God outside the ordinary course of nature. Such for example, were the signs and wonders of Our Lord in the Gospel, His walking over the waters, His miracles of healing, His feeding of the five thousand in the desert, His calling back of Lazarus from death to life. These are miracles; but this cannot mean that God has broken His own laws. He cannot be a disturbing influence in that which exists only through His power and is continued only through His Providence. God is not lawless, God is law. 'All things were made by Him and without Him was made nothing ' (John, i, 3). We should never think of a miracle (since to be a miracle at all it is something done by God) as a break in the world, an interference; rather as the fulfilment of a law. When man rears plants and fruits under glass in a house artificially heated, he is not interfering with nature, but using her; when God uses His Son to feed five thousand in the desert, He is not violating, but merely fulfilling His own laws.

III

A science perhaps that has misunderstood its own principle of observation and patient deduction, may cry out that miracles cannot happen. God has His repartee ready. His epigram is Lourdes. Miracles cannot happen. Does it matter whether they can or cannot? They certainly do happen. He challenges age after age, such scientists as would build their philosophy in too narrow a logic. Once the miracles that occurred in the lives of the Saints were denounced in the name of science as untrue; now in the same name they are accepted, but explained away. Science alters but the miracles remain. They are worked by God. They are outside the normal course of nature, but they have each their own purposes, and are operated in virtue of a law. Just as nervous excitement may enable a soldier, severely wounded, to go on fighting, and only when he sees his blood and realizes that he is badly hit, to collapse; just as a law of Nature enables mind to control matter, so God also in His own world controls and conquers its laws in virtue of other laws. By miracles we mean no more than this.

LAW

I

THERE is something majestic about the sound of the word law, and something exceedingly irritating. It is majestic because it calls up pictures of stately judges with scarlet robes and venerable wigs, looking so gravely out of family portraits or in the National Gallery, and with these pictures go, too, the remembrance of their sober and dignified judgements, their wise and austere diction, their careful arguments, their power to pronounce the death sentence with its awful ending: 'And may God have mercy on your soul'. Majesty, too, seems linked with it in English history, for despite occasional exceptions, the law has stood on the whole for the liberty of the subject and constitutional justice. Yet law conjures up not only majesty to our imagination, but sometimes galling restraint. It has done such irritating things, we think it cumbersome, gripped by the dead hand of the past, with its quotations from statutes and cases settled in far-off days under the rule of long-dead kings. Its stateliness looks majestic, but proves irritating. It is too majestic altogether and not human enough. It sentences the wrong people and dismisses the wrong people: some wretched woman is harried for murdering a child with which a dishonourable man has left her as a pledge of her constancy and his fickleness, while well-known and public swindlers elude for so long, sometimes finally, the unwieldy operations of the Courts. A judge may be most impressive, but a policeman can sometimes be exasperating.

II

We demand law and order, yet there is nothing under which we chafe more than law and order. The simple truth is that human nature is too moody a thing to fit in for long with regulations and injunctions. The law is fixed and dead; man is unstable and alive. Yet undoubtedly law is from God. By law we mean primarily the principles of justice revealed by God to us, either through faith or the native operations of the mind. A law implies a law-giver. It cannot be of itself.

We notice that motion has its laws, that vertebrates have certain inseparable characteristics, that light is conditioned, and thought, and numbers, and finance. These things we notice, trace, find endless proofs of; but the explanation of them is guesswork, an hypothesis which states but does not explain. Over all, then, we place God. God made the world, and gave to each thing in creation its number, weight and place.

III

It is a principle of creation, then, that things are true when they correspond to what God meant them to be (you recall, perhaps, the archetypes of Plato?), as a portrait is true, if it faithfully represent its subject. Now the same principle is to be applied not only to the laws of nature, but to the laws of men. Man was created by God for a certain purpose, to be guessed at by envisaging the nature given him by God. Further, besides the laws of his nature, he needs other laws, that he may live in peaceful society with his fellows. Laws are imposed because man is a sinner. Were he perfect, he would fulfil righteousness of himself. Because of wickedness or ignorance or thoughtlessness or perplexity he does the thing he should not; laws are to help the man to do the thing he should. For that very reason no law can hold him unless it be according to the law and nature of God. Anything against God is no law; it would be unjust, a violation of justice, a contradiction of man's purpose. Human positive laws then must be measured against the eternal principles of truth and justice; they must not oppose these, they need not refer to God or the faith, but they must not oppose the natural principles instilled into our hearts. Majestic or irritating as law may seem to us, according to our moods and our desires, the only view of it that really matters is that if it be law at all, it is divine.

Date Due			
'46			